LINUX
COMMAND LINE

The Simple and Powerful Guide to Master Shell Scripting For Intermediate Experts

David A. Williams

© Copyright 2019 by David A. Williams - All rights reserved.

This document is geared towards providing exact and reliable information in regards to the topic and issue covered. The publication is sold with the idea that the publisher is not required to render accounting, officially permitted, or otherwise, qualified services. If advice is necessary, legal or professional, a practiced individual in the profession should be ordered.

- From a Declaration of Principles which was accepted and approved equally by a Committee of the American Bar Association and a Committee of Publishers and Associations.

In no way is it legal to reproduce, duplicate, or transmit any part of this document in either electronic means or in printed format. Recording of this publication is strictly prohibited and any storage of this document is not allowed unless with written permission from the publisher. All rights reserved.

The information provided herein is stated to be truthful and consistent, in that any liability, in terms of inattention or otherwise, by any usage or abuse of any policies, processes, or directions contained within is the solitary and utter responsibility of the recipient reader. Under no circumstances will any legal responsibility or blame be held against the publisher for any reparation, damages, or monetary loss due to the information herein, either directly or indirectly.

Respective authors own all copyrights not held by the publisher.

The information herein is offered for informational purposes solely, and is universal as so. The presentation of the information is without contract or any type of guarantee assurance.

The trademarks that are used are without any consent, and the publication of the trademark is without permission or backing by the trademark owner. All trademarks and brands within this book are for clarifying purposes only and are the owned by the owners themselves, not affiliated with this document.

TABLE OF CONTENTS

INTRODUCTION 1

CHAPTER 1: WHAT IS SHELL? 3

CHAPTER 2: USING VARIABLES AND COMMENTS 7

CHAPTER 3: READ USER INPUT 12

CHAPTER 4: PASS ARGUMENTS TO SCRIPT 19

CHAPTER 5: IF STATEMENT 24

CHAPTER 6: FILE TEST OPERATORS 36

CHAPTER 7: APPEND TEXT FILE 44

CHAPTER 8: LOGICAL 'AND' AND 'OR' OPERATOR 49

CHAPTER 9: PERFORM ARITHMETIC OPERATIONS 57

CHAPTER 10: THE CASE STATEMENT 70

CHAPTER 11: ARRAY VARIABLES 79

CHAPTER 12: WHILE LOOPS 90

CHAPTER 13: UNTIL LOOPS 104

CHAPTER 14: FOR LOOPS 109

CHAPTER 15: SELECT LOOPS 120

CHAPTER 16: BREAK AND CONTINUE 125

CHAPTER 17: FUNCTIONS 130

CHAPTER 18: LOCAL VARIABLES 138

CHAPTER 19: READ ONLY COMMAND 149

CHAPTER 20: SIGNALS AND TRAPS 154

CHAPTER 21: HOW TO DEBUG SCRIPT 167

CONCLUSION 171

REFERENCES 172

Introduction

This guide contains proven steps and strategies on how to become a master in shell scripting in Linux using a command-line interface. Shell scripting is one of the primary skills in demand for Linux administrators, either a fresher or a professional. This book gives practical hands-on knowledge to start from basic to skilled Linux administrators. Whether you are new to the shell scripting world or you already have knowledge from our first guide for beginners, this book will give you a unique insight. Shell scripting is the only way with which you can automate maximum daily jobs with a very systematic approach saving your time and effort. After understanding the book and doing all the practical exercises given, your expertise will be at a much higher level. You will understand the concept of shells, how it works in the background, and what approaches to use to write a useful script.

The author of this book is an expert and professional in the industry and shares all knowledge that took them years to learn. This book is written for intermediate users, but if you do not have basic knowledge, the first few chapters will give you an overview and take you to the more skilled levels.

I'll cover the basics, including arguments, operators, arrays, loops, and much more, which any professional needs daily for Linux administration tasks. You will learn every topic from very basic to expert level exercises and get clarity on the logic used. This book will help you read and understand complex script and change it dynamically with expected results.

This book has more practical examples and works on the expectation that you have read our first book, "Shell Scripting For Beginners." If you are looking to get more knowledge on the basics, we recommend getting the first book in the series to understand the history and theory of shell scripting.

CHAPTER 1

What is Shell?

Unix shell interprets user commands which are directly executed by the user or by reading from a file known as the **shell script** or **shell program**.

Usage of shell—Please see the diagram below.

When the Linux machine is powered ON, first it loads its kernel. A kernel is an interface between hardware and the operating system. The kernel manages hardware resources like CPU, RAM, Input/Output devices to the application for any software to run. Any application needs to connect to the kernel to work. That is where the shell comes into the picture to connect the application to the kernel.

It is essential to know that shell script can be interpreted but cannot be compiled. When you write a shell script, the operating system interprets it, and there is no need to compile the shell script to execute it. There are multiple types of scripting options available.

Which Shell does your Operating System Support?

To check which shell type your operating system will support, check the/etc/shells file.

```
$ cat shells
/bin/ash
/bin/bash
/bin/csh
/bin/dash
/bin/sh
```

The above output of the command shows that the system can run shells – ash, bash, csh, dash, sh, and tcsh.

The 'sh' shell stands for the Bourne shell, which is the original shell still used on Unix or in Unix-like environments. The 'sh' was the first shell used in the Unix operating system.

Bash – it stands for Bourne Against the Shell and is the improved version of 'sh.' These days, bash is the standard GNU shell. It is intuitive and flexible. These days, this is the most commonly used shell in UNIX or LINUX based operating systems. They also use it in MacOS and Windows 10 environments.

To check about the location of your shell, you can check with the 'which' command. For example, you want to check the location of the bash shell in your operating system, run the below command.

```
$ which bash
/bin/bash
```

The output '/bin/bash' shows the location of the bash.

Now you have the required information about the bash; next, we will create our first script file.

Create the First Script File. Go to the directory location where you want to create the script. We are creating the file with a "touch" command. As a practice, the script file has an extension '.sh'. It is not a rule to have this extension, but when you use your editor, the editor will understand that this is a shell script file, and it displays an enhanced version.

```
$ touch hello.sh
$ ls -l
total 0
-rw-r--r-- 1 user1 users 0 Oct 30 20:35 hello.sh
```

In the example, we can see that the file owner has read-write permission, group, and others have read-only permission. The permission must be changed, so it is executable as a script. Below is the command to change the permissions of the file to executable only for the owner of the file.

```
$ chmod +x hello.sh
$ ls -al
total 0
drwxr-xr-x 2 user1 users 22 Oct 30 20:35 .
drwxr-xr-x 4 root  root  34 Oct 30 20:27 ..
-rwxr-xr-x 1 user1 users  0 Oct 30 20:35 hello.sh
```

Once we have created the file, next we write the script. You can use any editor, such as gedit, nano, vi/vim, etc. We are using vi for the purposes of this book.

The First Script

The first line in the script would be #!. These two characters will make the operating system understand that this is not a general ASCII text file, but a shell script. It gives an option to define which shell script you want to use and, by default, the system considers it a 'sh' script if #! is not there in the first line.

Next to #!, you need to give the path of the shell script you want to use. We commonly use bash scripting, so to use the bash script, the first line would be:

```
#! /bin/bash
```

Or you can write the location or the script you want to use after #!.

Our first script is simple using 'echo' command as below:

```
#! /bin/bash
```

```
echo "Hello World."
```

This script has now two lines, the first line to define the script and its location, and the second line is the command to execute - 'echo.'

Save the file, go to the command prompt, and execute the script as below using './'.

```
$ ./hello.sh
Hello World
```

The output has come to say 'Hello World'; that is what we expected the script to execute and print on the screen.

Summary: This is how we can check the scripts in our operating system, find the path of the script shell, set up permissions for the file and understand the first line of the script and the format in which to write it, and finally, how to execute the script.

CHAPTER 2

Using Variables and Comments

In the last chapter, we looked at creating and executing a new script. In this chapter, we will learn about comments and variables.

Comments

Comments are the lines of the code that are not executed by the script but are helpful to know some information about the executable lines. Any line in script started with a '#' becomes comment and would not be executed by the script.

Example

```
#! /bin/bash

# This is a comment
echo "Hello World."
```

Another way you can write a comment after the code is to put '#' after the command.

Example

```
#! /bin/bash

# This is a comment
echo "Hello World"  # This is also a comment
```

These are two ways we can use comments. Remember, comments are not executed as part of the script.

Variables

Variables are the containers that store data inside them. Whenever you define a variable, it stores some data. The variable could be a string, number, etc. There are two types of variables:

System Variables

In the Unix or Linux operating system creates system variables. There are pre-defined variables. As a standard convention, system variables are defined in upper case.

For example, in our hello.sh script, we can add a system variable, 'echo $BASH', to check the path of the shell for the user logged in. Now the script will look like this:

```
#! /bin/bash

# This is a comment
echo "Hello World"   # This is also a comment
```

echo $BASH

Now, when we execute the script, the output comes out like this:

```
$ ./hello.sh
Hello World
/bin/bash
```

This shows the path of bash scripts /bin/bash.

Let's practice more examples to be familiar with system variables. In the same script, let's add three more system variables:

BASH_VERSION: To display the bash version
HOME: To display the home directory
PWD: To display the present working directory

Now the script will look like this.

```
#! /bin/bash

# This is a comment
echo "Hello World"    # This is also a comment

echo $BASH
echo $BASH_VERSION
echo $HOME
echo $PWD
```

When we execute the script, the output will come like this.

```
$ ./hello.sh
Hello World
/bin/bash
```

`4.4.23(1)-release`	← Output of echo $BASH_VERSION that is the version of Bash in system
`/home/user1`	← Output of echo $HOME, that is the home directory of the user
`/home`	← Output of echo $PWD, that is current directory from where the script is executed.

Below you will find a list of some common system variables.

User-Defined Variables

The user-defined variables are created and maintained by users like us. As a general practice, these are defined in lower case, but there is no rule which stops you from writing these variables in upper case. The variable's name should contain alphabetic and not numeric values. If any variable name starts with a number, then the script may execute with no error, but the output may be incorrect.

To define this variable, write the name of the variable - that could be anything and then give it a value. Separate the name of the variable and its value with symbol '=.' The 'echo' command can display the value of the variable by putting the '$' symbol before the variable name.

For example, our hello.sh script lets us add a user-defined variable "name" and its value as John. Before giving its value, we can also type a text string and use the value in between the strings as in the example below.

The script will look like this:

```
#! /bin/bash

# This is a comment
echo "Hello World"    # This is also a comment

#Below are the system-defined variables.
echo $BASH
echo $BASH_VERSION
echo $HOME
echo $PWD

# Below is the user-defined variable
name=John
echo $name
```

Now, when you execute the script, having system variables and the new user-defined variable, the output will be displayed as below:

```
$ ./hello.sh
Hello World
My shell is /bin/bash
My Shell version name is 4.4.23(1)-release
My home directory is /home/user1
My present working directory is /home
John
```

Similarly, text string can also be used in system-defined variables, also as below. Now the script will look like this:

```
#! /bin/bash

# This is a comment
echo "Hello World"    # This is also a comment

#Below are the system-defined variables
echo My shell is $BASH
echo My Shell version name is $BASH_VERSION
echo My home directory is $HOME
echo My present working directory is $PWD

# Below are user-defined variables
name=John
echo The name is $name
```

and when we execute the script, the output will look like below:

```
$ ./hello.sh
Hello World
My shell is /bin/bash
My Shell version name is 4.4.23(1)-release
My home directory is /home/user1
My present working directory is /home
The name is John
```

Summary: You learned how to use comments and variables, system variables, and user-defined variables in the shell script.

CHAPTER 3

Read User Input

In this chapter, you will learn how we read inputs from the inputs given from your terminal in your script. To get some input from the keyboard, use the read command. This takes input from the keyboard and assigns it as a value for the variable. This is a user-interactive way to get the input of a variable. In a nutshell, when we execute the script, it prompts us for some value from the user, and this input becomes the value of that variable.

Let's see an example in the script that will ask you to enter a name. The name we enter will become the value of the variable, and finally, echo will display the name given. The script will look like this:

```
#! /bin/bash

echo "Enter the name : "        ← Message to enter a name

read name                        ← Read command prompts the user to
                                   enter the name, and this will become
                                   the value of variable

echo "The name entered is : $name" ← Display the name
                                     entered for the variable in the input
                                     above.
```

Now when we execute the script, the system will wait for the 'value' input after the 'read' command.

```
$ ./hello.sh

Enter the name :          ← Displays the 1st line of script

John                      ← Input typed by user

The name entered is: John    ← Displays 3rd line of script
                                with output as 'John', the value given
                                in line 2.
```

Add Multiple Variables

There may be a situation when you want to add multiple variables in the same command. It can be done by adding multiple variable names after the "read" command. A space should separate each variable. To display the multiple values in output, the output line must also have all variable names defined for which we want to see the output.

For example, in the previous script, we wanted the user to input three names and display the same in output. In that case, the script would look like this:

```
#! /bin/bash



echo "Enter the names : "
read name1 name2 name3
echo "The Names entered are : $name1, $name2, $name3"
```

And when we execute the script, the output looks like this:

```
$ ./hello.sh
Enter the names :
```

```
John Mak Adam
```
 ← All inputs should be in the same line, separated by space.

```
The names entered are: John, Mak, Adam
```

In the above example, when we execute the script, the script prompts us to enter that name and that prompt goes on the next line. Sometimes we would need to get the prompt on the same line as a string. In that scenario, we place the input on the same line where the query was prompted. Sometimes is it necessary to have the prompt on the same line as the string. By adding a flag '-p' after 'read' command, this can be done.

For example, in the example below:

We make the first line the system aware of the shell type being used.

The second line is where the 'read' command is running with a –p flag, so the system should prompt the value on the same line, and then "user_var" is the variable name.

The third line, 'echo', will display the text 'username' with the variable value, entered the second line as a value of "user_var." The script will look like this:

```
#! /bin/bash


read -p 'username : ' user_var
echo "Entered username : $user_var"
```

The script will execute as below:

```
$ ./hello.sh

username : john
```
                                    ← System prompt input in same line

```
Entered username: john
```
 ← Output displayed as the input given in the previous step.

Silent Input

Sometimes there is a requirement to have silent input. Silent means it does not display the input on the screen, like passwords. When we type a password on the system, we prefer it that the system does not display it on=screen for security reasons. We can do this by adding the flag '-s.' Let's understand it in the example given below.

In the previous script, let's add "pass_var" as a variable to enter the password, and it should be silent. So in this case, we have to use two flags,

-p to prompt on the same line
-s to keep the input silent.

Now the script will look like this:

```
#! /bin/bash

read -p 'username : ' user_var
read -sp 'password : ' pass_var
echo "Entered username : $user_var"
echo "Entered password : $pass_var"
```

The output shown below will come when we execute the script. The password entered manually in this example is 12345. The output will look like this.

```
$ ./hello.sh
username: john
password: Entered username: john
Entered password: 12345
```

Entered password looks silent, but the system has captured it as the value in the "pass_var" variable. With the echo command to display the password variable as '12345'. Also, you can see after the password, in the same line, it displays the output of the variable

'Entered username,' which does not look meaningful. It needs a correction to display the outputs of 'echo' in the next line.

To fix this, you can add a blank 'echo' to the next line of the 'password' variable. The script will look like below:

```
#! /bin/bash

read -p 'username : ' user_var
read -sp 'password : ' pass_var
echo
echo "Entered username : $user_var"
echo "Entered password : $pass_var"
```

Now execute the script, the output will look like this:

```
$ ./hello.sh
username : john
password :
Entered username : john
Entered password : 12345
```

Everything looks fine now.

Array

There are situations when inputs are in thousands; the time needed to set the values of all variables individually will not be a viable solution. In that case, when 'array' comes into the picture. An array can store multiple values by setting up the index number. Korn shell and bash shell start index numbers from 0. In the format below, this array is displayed.

{$<variable name>[<index number>]}

The advance level course will cover more about the details of an array.

For now, let's understand how we can create arrays and how to display the values of the index of an array.

In case you want to allow users to enter multiple inputs and you want to save those inputs into an array, '-a' flag will help to get it done.

Let's create a script where after the 'read' command, we will set '-a' flag which will set up an array. After '-a' whatever variable name you give it here, it will be an array, and also, it will allow the user to enter multiple values.

```
#! /bin/bash

echo "Enter Names : "
read -a names
echo "Names : " ${names[0]}, ${names[2]}
```

In the script with the read command, we have set '-a' flag, which means we can give multiple input values as input. The last line is doing an echo for the index element number at number 0 and number 2. This means it will display the output of the value entered 1st, and the 3rd one. Let's execute the script and enter four values to get clarity. The variable is started with and closed with the { and } brackets, the index number is between the square bracket [and].

Now let's execute the script and see how the output looks.

```
$ ./hello.sh
Enter Names :
john mak adam hary
Names: john, adam
```

In this example, we have given input of 4 names for the array 'names' separated by a space. The last line shows the value of the elements of the index created in the array as the first name 'john' and third name 'adam.'

REPLY

There is another variable known as 'REPLY' which is a default variable with the read command. What happens when there is no variable written in front of the 'read' command, when the default variable 'REPLY' works, it just displays the inputs given to read the command.

```
#! /bin/bash

echo "Enter Names : "
read
echo "Names: " $REPLY
```

When we execute the script

```
$ ./hello.sh
Enter Names :
john mak adam hary
Names:  john mak adam hary
$
```

We set the input of 4 names as the value of the variable REPLY, and the output is the same as the input.

CHAPTER 4

Pass Arguments to Script

In the last chapter, we looked at reading parameters. There are requirements when you need to pass the arguments to the script. Arguments are the inputs to the standard input to get a desired filtered output. An example when we write ls /home, that means 'ls' is the command and '/home' is an argument to show the listing of files in /home directory. Similarly, command 'ls / /home' now has two arguments '/' and '/home'. In this chapter, we will discover how arguments are passed to a script.

In the script shown below, after 'echo,' the $1, $2, and $3 means there would be three arguments that would be the inputs. These three variables will store the three values that will be entered as input variables.

```
#! /bin/bash

echo $1 $2 $3
```

Now to execute the script, we will give three arguments along with the script, and in the output, we should see these three values printed.

```
$ ./hello.sh John Mak Tom
John Mak Tom
```

We saw that we got an output for $1, $2, and $3 variable as John, Mak, and Tom, respectively. But in input apart from these 3 inputs, there is another 4th variable in the input that is ./hello.sh, that has not come in output. This is the variable at 0th number. Since in our script we have not written $0, it does not print this. Now let's add $0 to the script, and then we should see ./hello.sh in the output.

Now the script has become

```
#! /bin/bash

echo $0 $1 $2 $3
```

Let's execute and see the output.

```
$ ./hello.sh John Mak Tom
./hello.sh John Mak Tom
```

We expected this, now we have got the 0th variable - ./hello.sh also in the output.

Now you need to understand how you can parse the arguments whatever you give to your script as an array. To do this in the same script, let's add a variable 'args.' There is a default variable in which these arguments go in as an array, and that is "@." To define an array, you need to write $@ in a bracket - ($@). '$@' stores your arguments as an array; these arguments will be the values of the variable 'args.' Once these are set, we can print the output with the 'echo' command. To print the output, we will use the format of the array to display the values of the variables. There you can define that array 'args' should print the value of which the index number.

Now the script will become as below:

```
#! /bin/bash

echo $0 $1 $2 $3
args=("$@")
```

```
echo ${args[0]} ${args[1]} ${args[2]} ${args[3]}
```

Once the script is executed the output looks like this

```
$ ./hello.sh John Mak Tom
./hello.sh John Mak Tom
John Mak Tom
```

In the first line, we executed the script with the same three arguments. The second line shows the output of arguments as the 1st command (echo $0 $1 $2 $3), and the third line shows the output of array (args=("$@")). Now the critical point to note here is, in the second line, the index 0 was ./hello.sh, and when it becomes the argument for an array, the index 0 was John. For arguments, the script name 0 index did not print.

Therefore, the default variable starts from 0, where 0 is the variable for the script name. But when you assign them as an array, then the 0th index will be the first argument similarly 1st index will be the second argument, 2nd index will be the third argument and so on. That means if we delete '${args[3]}' from the script, the result will be the same. Let's try this:

```
#! /bin/bash

echo $0 $1 $2 $3
args=("$@")
echo ${args[0]} ${args[1]} ${args[2]}
```

Now, still, the output is the same.

```
$ ./hello.sh John Mak Tom
./hello.sh John Mak Tom
John Mak Tom
```

If you want to display all the values of the array, then you can echo the $@ variable. This is the default variable that will show all the arguments. Now in the script, let's comment on the echo line and add a new echo line with $@ to display all the arguments.

```
#! /bin/bash

echo $0 $1 $2 $3

args=("$@")
# echo ${args[0]} ${args[1]} ${args[2]} ${args[3]}
echo $@
```

Now let's execute the script with the same arguments, the output will show all arguments.

```
$ ./hello.sh John Mak Tom
./hello.sh John Mak Tom
John Mak Tom
```

And yes, it did. This shows it saved all the arguments in the default variable @

Sometimes there is a need to know the number of arguments passed to the script, a default variable for this that is '# can do this. The "#" variable is a default variable to show the number of arguments passed to the script.

In our script, we have passed three arguments, so when we made the changed to the script by adding this variable, it should display the number 3. Let's add this variable to the script. The script will look like this:

```
#! /bin/bash

echo $0 $1 $2 $3
args=("$@")
# echo ${args[0]} ${args[1]} ${args[2]} ${args[3]}
echo $@

echo $#
```

When we execute the script, the output will be

```
$ ./hello.sh John Mak Tom
./hello.sh John Mak Tom
John Mak Tom
3
```

Now here we can see the number 3, which shows that three numbers of arguments passed to the script as input.

These are the few ways you can pass on the arguments to the shell script.

CHAPTER 5

if Statement

In this chapter, we will learn about the "if" statement. If you are familiar with any programing language, then you may know that an if statement can test some condition and if the condition is true, then the code will be executed; otherwise, it goes to the else condition or is not executed. Let's know how we can use the "if" statement in our script.

How to Write the if in a Statement

In the script, once the "if" condition is there, it will have a square bracket that will enclose the condition. There should be a space for text in the beginning, and towards the end of the square bracket, or else the script will give an error. The text written in. The next line follows the keyword "then." The next line says if the condition is true, then follow the statement, and once the statement is executed, then the last line will have "fi" for the end of the 'if' statement.

Below is the basic syntax of 'if' statement how it will look

```
if [condition]
then
     Statement
fi
```

Below is the list of the operator that integers and string comparison will use:

```
-eq - is equal to - if ["$a" -eq "$b"]
-ne - is not equal to - if [ "$a" -ne "$b" ]
-gt - is greater than - if [ "$a" -gt "$b" ]
-ge - is greater than or equal to - if [ "$a" -ge "$b"]
-lt - is less than - if [ "$a" -le "$b" ]
-le - is less than or equal to - if [ "$a" -le "$b" ]
< - is less than - (("$a" < "b"))
<= - is less than or equal to - (("$a" <= "$b"))
> - is greater than - (("$a" > "$b"))
>= -  is greater than or equal to - (("$a" >= "$b"))
```

String Comparisons

```
= - is equal to - If [ "$a" == "b" ]
== - is equal to - If [ "$a" == "b" ]
!= - is not equal to - if [ "$a" != "b" ]
< - is less than, in ASCII alphabetical order - if [[ "$a" < "b" ]]
> - is greater than, in ASCII alphabetical order - if [[ "$a" > "b" ]]
-z - String is null, that is, it has zero length
```

This example is used to understand the first operation 'equal to' (-eq). In the condition, we can put some parameters to compare the number. For that, we will use comparison operators with an integer. For comparison, we will use equality, non-equality, greater than, less than, greater than and equal to, less than and equal to, etc.

For this example, we are setting up a variable "unit" with its value as 10. We will use 'equal to–eq' as a comparison operator. After giving the operator, provide a number, in our example, we are giving number 9. Now we know that the condition is not true as ten is not equal to 9. In "then" we are putting an echo, that condition is true. In our case, the condition is not true; it will print to nothing in the output.

The script will look like below:

```
#! /bin/bash

unit=10
if [$unit -eq 9 ]
then
   echo "condition is true."
fi
```

Now let's execute the script.

```
$ ./hello.sh
$
```

As expected, nothing printed in output as the condition is not true. To make the condition true, we will change the number from 9 to 10, and then the condition becomes true.

Now the script will look like this:

```
#! /bin/bash

unit=10

if [ $unit -eq 10 ]
then
   echo "condition is true."
fi
```

Let's execute the script.

```
$ ./hello.sh
condition is true
```

Now it prints "condition is true." To get more familiar with this, you can try other expressions mentioned in the table. Below are more examples to get good clarity on using comparisons.

For expression–ne, that is 'not equal to' and Let's use 9 in the 'if' statement. That means the condition is true as nine is not equal to 10. Let's change the script and execute it.

```
#! /bin/bash

unit=10

if [ $unit -ne 9 ]
then
   echo "condition is true."
fi
```

Let's execute the script.

```
$ ./hello.sh
condition is true
```

It works well.

Expression –gt – greater than. Now in our script, ten is greater than 9, which means the condition is true, so we should get the same output. Let's change the expression in the "if" statement and execute the script.

```
#! /bin/bash

unit=10

if [ $unit -gt 9 ]
then
   echo "condition is true."
fi
```

Let's execute the script.

```
$ ./hello.sh
condition is true
```

Similarly, you can try all the operators. As you can see in the table. For angle bracket symbols - < and >, the format is different. For angle brackets, which side the side which angle bracket opens has to be the bigger number, for example, the right format to write is 10 > 9. Here the angle bracket opens toward 10, as that is a bigger number. To fulfill the condition, we need to follow this rule.

Now we are changing the script with an angle bracket and see how the script works.

```
#! /bin/bash

unit=10

if [ $unit > 9 ]
then
   echo "condition is true."
fi
```

Now let's execute the script:

```
$ ./hello.sh
condition is true
```

One more change in the 'if' statement. In place of the square bracket, we will put double parentheses, and it should work.

Let's change the script with double parentheses and see the result.

```
#! /bin/bash

unit=10

if (( $unit > 9 ))
then
   echo "condition is true."
fi
```

Now let's execute the script:

```
$ ./hello.sh
condition is true
```

Next, we will see the greater than and equal to expression (>=) in the script and see how it works. In our script, this condition is also true.

Make the changes script; it looks like as below:

```
#! /bin/bash

unit=10

if (( $unit >= 9 ))
then
   echo "condition is true."
fi
```

Now let's execute the script:

```
$ ./hello.sh
condition is true
```

Similarly, you can try the other integer expressions.

To compare the string expression, the conditions work in the same way; only the format will change. For expression equal to (= or ==), not equal to (!=), in the 'if' syntax the conditions go in the square brackets. The angled brackets (< or >) are used for alphabetical order.

In our script, now we will use alphabet expressions. To use the alphabetic expressions, we will put square brackets in the 'if' statement. We are using the value for variable 'unit' as abc and in 'if' condition, let's put the value also 'abc.'

Now the script will as below:

```
#! /bin/bash

unit=abc
if [ $unit == abc ]
then
   echo "condition is true."
fi
```

Now let's execute the script:

```
$ ./hello.sh
condition is true
```

Let's change the value in the condition value for 'if' from abc to abcd, which is not a true condition.

Now the script will as below:

```
#! /bin/bash

unit=abc
if [ $unit == abcd ]
then
   echo "condition is true."
fi
```

Execute the script; the output should be blank:

```
$ ./hello.sh
$
```

The result is as expected.

In this above example for the string, we have used double equal signs (==), even if we use the single equals to sign, that will also work. Normally in programming languages like C++, Java, etc., uses only ==, but in scripting, it works both = or ==.

Another condition string is not equal to (!=). We are now changing the script to check this condition. Changing the condition for an if statement from abc to abcd. The script will be now as below:

```
#! /bin/bash

unit=abc

if [ $unit != abcd ]
then
   echo "condition is true."
fi
```

The condition is true, so when we execute the script, we should get the success message.

```
$ ./hello.sh
condition is true
```

This looks perfect.

If you want to check the alphabetical order, angular brackets can do that (< or >). To check this in the script, we are changing the unit value to 'a' and putting 'b' as a condition value in the 'if' statement using an angular bracket with an open side towards 'b.' Here one more rule will be applied now when there are integers to compare with angular symbols; then double brackets are used. Now, in this case, we are using alphabets to compare, so we need to use double square brackets. If the same brackets are used for the alphabet script, it won't work and end up with an error.

Script will be as below:

```
#! /bin/bash

unit=a

if [[ $unit < b ]]
```

```
then
    echo "condition is true."
fi
```

In alphabetical order, 'a' comes before 'b', that means the condition is true. When the script is executed, the message will come.

```
$ ./hello.sh
condition is true
```

In summary, keep the conditions shown below in mind.

Square brackets [or] are used in comparison operators with integers with eq, ne, gt, ge, lt, and le operations.

Double parentheses ((or)) are used where integer comparison using angular brackets < or >.

Square brackets [or] are used to compare equality of the strings with operators =, == or !=.

Double square brackets [[or]] are used when a string comparison is done with angular brackets < or >.

Else

When learning about the if statement, we learned one other condition which is 'then'. There is another condition you can use which is the 'else' condition. In the 'if' statement, the if condition met the 'if' expression, the script executes the command defined in 'then,' but what will happen if the condition is false, then we may need to run some other command, 'else' condition does that. In short, if the condition matches, then the command defined in 'then' will execute. If it does not meet the condition, the script will run the command defined in 'else.' Examples illustrated below will give more clarity.

We will add 'else' condition in our existing script now.

After we define the condition in 'then,' in the next line, we will add the 'else' condition with a next line with the command to execute it. Also, we will change the 'if' statement to check if 'a' is equal to 'b.' In this script, the script will check first if this condition is true or not; it is not. Now the script will ignore the 'then' condition and directly run the command written in the 'else' condition.

The script will look like below:

```
#! /bin/bash

unit=a

if [[ $unit == b ]]
then
   echo "condition is true."
else
   echo "condition is false."
fi
```

Script will give the below output once executed:

```
$ ./hello.sh
condition is false
```

This is what we expected. So the 'else' condition will execute if the condition is not true.

If you want, you can evaluate multiple conditions, and based on those multiple conditions, the statement will take action. In that case, 'elif' does it. This is another way with which we can use the else condition with the 'if' statement. In the script, after writing the 'then' statement on the next line, we write the 'elif' statement. In case the script does not execute the 'then' condition, in that case, the script will look for code written in 'elif.' We elaborate on this in the example below of our running script.

In the example, we have kept 'unit' variable with value 'a' and in 'if' expression we are checking if variable 'unit' is equal to 'b.'

```
if [[ $unit == b ]]
```

In the 'then' statement, we are changing the statement of echo to 'condition b is true.'

```
then
   echo "condition b is true."
```

Next line to 'then,' we will add a new condition 'elif,' like 'if' we will write the 'elif' statement also to check if the variable 'unit' has the value 'a.' And under 'elif', we will add another line of 'then' and give the statement as 'condition a is true' if condition matches in 'elif.

```
elif [[ $unit == a ]]
then
   echo "condition a is true."
```

If this is also not true, then finally, the script will execute the 'else' condition.

```
else
   echo "condition is false."
```

Now the script will look like below:

```
#! /bin/bash

unit=a

if [[ $unit == b ]]
then
   echo "condition b is true"
elif [[ $unit == a ]]
then
   echo "condition a is true."
else
```

```
    echo "condition is false."
fi
```

Now let's execute the script.

```
$ ./hello.sh
condition a is true
```

Which looks good. In the output, we got the code executed by the 'then' statement under 'elif' because the 'unit' variable is equal to 'a.' In summary, the sequence of code execution will go like this:

The script will first read the condition of 'if', and it will check code under 'then'; if it matches, it will execute the code for 'then.' In case that doesn't match, the script will check for the 'elif' condition, and code executed for 'then' under 'elif.' If that also doesn't match, then the script will reach 'else' and execute code under 'else.'

Summary: In this chapter, you learned

If, elif and else statement and how to use in scripts.

CHAPTER 6

File Test Operators

In this chapter, we will learn how to use 'if' statements in 'File test operators.'

Mostly when you are writing a shell script, you are dealing with the files. There would be situations when you want to check if the file exists or not, whether there is a regular file, block special file or character special file, and many other options you can check with File test operators. Let's learn how to use those conditions.

We will understand step by step of the script now.

The First line is to define the shell used in our case; it is bash

`#! /bin/bash`

Second line to write the statement with echo

`echo -e "Enter the name of the file : \c"`

`\c` will make the script to prompt the next input on the same line.

`-e` will make echo command to make aware that inside the statement of echo '`\c`' is not normal text, but this is a switch. So when 'echo' command is executed, then '`\c`' should not be printed as a text.

The **Third Line** is having 'read' command to read a variable file_name. This will be the variable name for the filename to check.

```
read file_name
```

In the **Fourth Line,** we will use 'if' expression; the expression will be in a square bracket as a rule. In brackets, a flag –e is used. –e flag will check if the file exists or not. After –e, we will write the variable 'file_name.'

```
if [ -e $file_name ]
```

The **Fifth Line** will define 'then'.

```
then
```

The **Sixth Line** will execute if the condition is true and echo the message that file_name is found.

```
echo "$file_name found"
```

The **Seventh Line** will write the 'else' condition

```
else
```

The **Eighth Line** will execute if the condition is not met and echo the message that file_name not found.

```
echo "$file_name not found."
```

The **Ninth Line** will end the script by 'fi.'

Now the script will look like below:

```
#! /bin/bash

echo -e "Enter the name of the file : \c"
read file_name
if [ -e $file_name ]
then
   echo "$file_name found"
```

```
else
   echo "$file_name not found."
fi
```

Now let's execute the script. When we execute, the second line having 'echo' command will prompt for the file name on the same line. In our example, we are giving a random file name 'test' which does not exist in the present working directory. That means condition will not meet, and that will make 'else' condition to execute.

Below we have shown the script executed and gave the file name as 'test', after the message, we have checked the existence of the filename in the current directory, which is not there.

```
$ ./hello.sh
Enter the name of the file : test
"test not found"
$ pwd
/home/user1
$ ls
hello.sh
$
```

Now let's create a file name 'test' with touch command and execute the script again.

```
$ touch test
$ ls
hello.sh   test
$ ./hello.sh
Enter the name of the file : test
"test found"
```

Now in the script code defined in 'then' statement is executed as the file is existing now.

Flag –e is the one that validates the existence of the file in the 'if' statement.

38

To check if the input name given is the regular file or not, '-f' flag will do that. We will change our script by changing flag –e to –f in the 'if' statement. The script will look as below:

```
#! /bin/bash

echo -e "Enter the name of the file : \c"
read file_name
if [ -f $file_name ]
then
   echo "$file_name found"
else
   echo "$file_name not found."
Fi
```

Now let's execute, and we will input the same filename; we know that 'test' is a regular file as we have created it with touch command. Now the condition is true.

```
$ ./hello.sh
Enter the name of the file : test
"test found"
```

We have the expected output.

Next, if we want to check if the directory exists, -d flag can do that. In our script, we are changing the flag from –f to –d. Also, we are changing the variable name to 'dir_name', to avoid the confusion of the names, we can also use though same variable name.

Now the script will look as below:

```
#! /bin/bash

echo -e "Enter the name of the directory : \c"
read dir_name
if [ -d $dir_name ]
then
   echo "$dir_name found"
```

```
else
   echo "$dir_name not found."
Fi
```

When we execute the script, it will prompt to enter a directory name; we will give input as 'dir.' With this name, no directory exists, so the code should execute the 'else' statement.

```
$ ./hello.sh
Enter the name of the directory: dir
"dir not found."
```

Now let's create a directory with the name 'dir' and execute the script again.

```
$ ls
hello.sh test
$ mkdir dir
$ ls
dir hello.sh   test
$ ./hello.sh
Enter the name of the directory: dir
"dir found"
```

So –d flag is to check for the existence of a directory.

Next, let's learn to check the type of files. There are two types of files, character special file, and a block special file. The character special file is normal ASCII text file, and the block special file is a binary file, for example, a picture, video, etc. Flag –b is used to check for block special file, and –c flag is used to check for character special file.

Flag –s is used to check if the file is empty or not. We will use this flag in our script to check if the file is empty or not.

We will change the script as below by adding the flag –s in the 'if' statement and changing variable back to file_name. Also, changing the text for 'then' and 'else' code. Condition 'then' will execute if the file is not empty and condition 'else' will execute if the file is empty.

Now the script will be as below:

```
#! /bin/bash

echo -e "Enter the name of the file : \c"
read file_name
if [ -s $file_name ]
then
   echo "$file_name not empty"
else
   echo "$file_name empty"
fi
```

Execute the script, and we will check for the file name 'test', which we know is empty.

```
$ ./hello.sh
Enter the name of the file: test
test empty
```

We can verify this with ls –l command to see the size of file

```
$ ls -l
total 4
drwxr-xr-x 2 user1 users    6 Nov 7 13:03 dir
-rwxr-xr-x 1 user1 users  163 Nov 7 13:35 hello.sh
-rw-r--r-- 1 user1 users    0 Nov 7 12:48 test
```

Here we can see that the size of the file is 0 bytes. Now we will add some content in the file using the 'cat' command, and after saving the file, we will check for the change in the size of the file.

```
$ cat > test
I have written data in this file.
$ ls -l
total 8
drwxr-xr-x 2 user1 users    6 Nov 7 13:03 dir
```

```
-rwxr-xr-x 1 user1 users 163 Nov  7 13:35 hello.sh
-rw-r--r-- 1 user1 users  33 Nov  7 13:42 test
```

We can see that the file 'test' has some data. Let's rerun the script and check for the same file name 'test' if this is empty or not.

```
$ ./hello.sh
Enter the name of the file : test
test not empty
```

Now it says 'test' not empty.

Below is the summary of some flags that you can define in 'if' expression to check on the property of the file.

```
-e: file exists or not
-f: file exists or not, and if the file exists, that
is a regular file or not.
-d: if the directory exists.
-b: To define the block special file
-c: To define the character special file.
-s: if the file is empty or not.
-r: if the file has read permission
-w: if the file has write permission
-x: if the file has execute permission
```

Nested 'if' condition in a script: In 'if' statement, there is an option to check for a single expression. Based on this expression, 'then and 'else' statements will take action. There will be an instance when, under a single 'if' expression, we can generate multiple sub-expressions and need to do more than 'then' and 'else' actions. This can be done by writing more 'if' statements. This is shown in the example below. We have added more 'if' statements into our existing script. In this chapter, we explain only the concept; the next chapter will show the usage with the example.

Example: we want to check if the filename we will give exists, and if it exists, then how can we write the option to check more conditions on file.

```
#! /bin/bash

echo -e "Enter the name of the file : \c"
read file_name
if [ -f $file_name ]
then
        if [ -w $file_name ]
        then
        else
        fi
else
   echo "$file_name not exists"
fi
```

CHAPTER 7

Append Text File

In the last chapter we learned about test operators in shell scripting. In this chapter we will merge the knowledge that we have gained in the last sections that are 'if' conditions and file test operators. We will learn how to write the text in a new file and how to append some text in a file that already exists and have data in it.

To understand this with an example, we will use some part of the script we have in the last chapter, and we will change it. Like in the script, it first prompts to write a file name, then in 'if' statement we will put –f flag to check whether file exists and is a test file. If the system validates that that file exists, next, we will check if the file and write permission to write some text in the file or not. If write permission is there, we will write into the file; otherwise, the script will send the message that there is no write permission.

We are doing the following changes in our last script:

- In 'if' statement putting flag –f to check for existence.

    ```
    if [ -f $file_name ]
    ```

- If the file exists, then we will check for write permission on this file. For that in 'then', we will add one more 'if' statement.

- In the new 'if' statement, add flag –w to check if the file has write permission. Next to –w, there will be the file_name variable.

  ```
  then
          if [ -w $file_name ]
  ```

- If write permission is there, the script will move to 'then,' under 'then' execute two commands. The command 'echo' to type some text and the 'cat' command, which will write the text in the file. In the 'cat' command, we are using the double angle brackets (>>) to append the file. If we use a single angle bracket (>), then it will overwrite the data. Next to angle brackets, there will be variable file_name, the file to be appended.

  ```
  then
      echo "Type some text data. To quit press ctrl+d"
      cat >> $file_name
  ```

- Next, we will maintain the 'else' section with 'echo' command to type that file does not have write permissions.

  ```
  else
    echo "This File does not have write permission."
  ```

- Now the 'then' and 'else' conditions are written, we will close the nested 'if' section by 'fi.'

- The next line will define the 'else' section with 'echo' command saying '$file_name does not exist'

  ```
  else
    echo "$file_name does not exist"
  ```

- Last, the script will be closed by 'fi.

Script will like below:

```
#! /bin/bash

echo -e "Enter the name of the file : \c"
read file_name
if [ -f $file_name ]
then
       if [ -w $file_name ]
       then
          echo "Type some text data. To quit press ctrl+d"
          cat >> $file_name
       else
          echo "This file does not have write permission."
       fi
else
   echo "$file_name not exists"
fi
```

Now execute the script. The file name we will give now to append is 'abc,' which does not exist.

```
$ ./hello.sh
Enter the name of the file : abc
abc doesn't exist
$ ls
dir hello .sh
```

Since the file does not exist, we will create the file by 'touch' command. By default, new file created with owner write permissions. To test our script, we will remove the write permission using command chmod command with the flag –w. –w will remove the write permission from the file.

```
$ touch abc
$ ls -al abc
-rw-r--r-- 1 user1 users     0 Nov  7 18:56 abc
```

```
$ chmod -w abc
$ ls -al abc
-r--r--r-- 1 user1 users     0 Nov  7 18:56 abc
```

Now we can see that write permission is removed from the file. Once again, we will run our script.

```
$ ./hello.sh
Enter the name of the file : abc
This file does not have write permission
```

The script has worked well and gave "This file does not have write permission" as we have removed it. Now giving back the write permission with 'chmod +w' command.

```
$ chmod +w abc
$ ls -al abc
-rw-r--r-- 1 user1 users 0 Nov  7 18:56 abc
```

The write permission to file 'abc' is back. Now let's execute the script again, this time we should be able to write to the file, as all conditions meet now, the file exists and is a regular text file which is checked by –f flag and last file have write permissions.

```
$ ./hello.sh
Enter the name of the file : abc
Type some text data. To quit press ctrl+d
Let's write some data - Hello World! ← After this we
pressed ctrl+d
$
```

After pressing ctrl+d, we will come back to the prompt. Now let's check if we have got the text written is there in the file 'abc.' We will check the content of the 'abc' file with the cat command.

```
$ ls -la abc
-rw-r--r-- 1 user1 users 38 Nov  7 19:10 abc ← File
has got some data
$ cat abc
```

```
Let's write some data - Hello World!
$
```

We have checked that the data written is there now. Next, let's check to append the file. For that, we will rerun the script and add more text. The added text should not overwrite the data but add the line after the previous line added.

```
$ ./hello.sh
Enter the name of the file : abc
Type some text data. To quit press ctrl+d
Shell Scripting course
$ cat abc
Let's write some data - Hello World!
Shell Scripting course
$
```

This looks perfect. The text has been appended in the file and not overwritten.

Summary: We have learned how to use nested 'if' conditions and different scenarios on how to append the file with a script.

CHAPTER 8

Logical 'AND' and 'OR' Operator

In this chapter, we will see how to use 'AND' and 'OR' operator with the if statement.

AND Operators

Let's say there is a requirement to write two or more expressions with the 'if' statement; in that case, we use the AND operator. When we use the 'AND' operator, then the script will validate all expressions to give a successful message that is defined in 'then.' If any condition is not validated, the script will execute code defined in 'else'. Until now we have learned how to write the condition with the 'if' statement. Now to write the second condition, we will use the 'AND' operator.

There are three ways with which an 'AND' operator can be used.

1. Two expressions are written in square brackets, and these brackets are separated by double '&' symbols, as shown below.

    if [expression 1] && [expression 2]

2. Two expressions are written in square brackets. The two '&' symbols shown above will be replaced by –a flag. –a stands

for AND. If you want to use a square bracket, you can use –a. This is shown below:

if [expression 1 –a expression 2]

3. You can use double square brackets to start and close the 'if' statement, and expressions are separated with double && symbol to define AND conditions. It is shown below:

if [[expression 1 && expression 2]]

Let's understand AND operation this with an example.

Suppose we have a student, and we need to test his age. We need to test in such a way that his age should be greater than 18 years and less than 30 years. How do we do it? Let's create the script.

By default first line is to mention the shell. Then we are assigning a variable 'age' with value 18. Now we will write the 'if' expression with a condition.

```
#! /bin/bash

age=25
```

Since we have to check two conditions, condition 1, the age has to be greater than 18 years and condition 2, that the age should be less than 30 years.

Expressions will be written in separate square brackets with 'if' statements. The first bracket will have the condition to check the variable '$age', if its value is greater than (-gt), number 18. In the second condition, we check that the variable $age is less than (-lt) number 30. The symbol '&&' will separate these brackets.

```
if [ $age -gt 18 ] && [ $age -lt 30 ]
```

Next, we will mention in 'then' and 'else' if the condition is a success or not.

If the condition is true, in that case, 'then' script will execute 'echo' code "valid age."

```
then
        echo "Valid age."
```

If the condition is not true, in that case, the 'else' script will execute 'echo' code "age not valid."

```
else
        echo "Age not valid"
```

In the last line, we will end the 'if' script with 'fi.'

The script will look like this:

```
#! /bin/bash

age=25
if [ $age -gt 18 ] && [ $age -lt 30 ]
then
        echo "Valid age."
else
        echo "Age not valid"
fi
```

Let's execute the script

```
$ ./hello.sh
Valid age
```

Since 25 falls between 18 and 30, and both expressions met the condition, the script executes the code mention in 'then' statement and displays 'Valid age'. Now let's change the number from 25 to 50 in the script, which is out of conditions range set.

```
#! /bin/bash

age=50
if [ $age -gt 18 ] && [ $age -lt 30 ]
```

```
then
        echo "Valid age."
else
        echo "Age not valid"
fi
```

Execute the script again

```
$ ./hello.sh
Age not valid
```

Now what happened in the 2nd case is that the first condition was true; age is greater than 18, but it is not meeting the second condition that the age has to be less than 30; that's why code written in 'else' executes.

If you want to change the format of 'AND' condition by using the single square bracket, that will also give the same result. Then the script will look as below:

```
#! /bin/bash

age=50
if [ $age -gt 18 -a  $age -lt 30 ]
then
        echo "Valid age."
else
        echo "Age not valid"
fi
```

If you execute the script, the result will be the same.

The third way to write the same script with double square brackets and the AND operations will be defined by &&. So we will replace – a with &&. The script will look as below.

```
#! /bin/bash

age=50
```

```
if [[ $age -gt 18 && $age -lt 30 ]]
then
        echo "Valid age."
else
        echo "Age not valid"
fi
```

OR Operators

In this section, we will learn about 'OR' logical operators and how to use them.

In AND operator, the 'if' statement checks for all expressions, and all expressions should be true after that only it moves to 'then.' In OR operator, 'if' statement checked for all expressions, and if any expressions are true, it will validate and move to 'then.' In case none on the conditions are true, it will go to 'else.'

We will use the same script which we have used in AND operator. Now, in this case, out of two expressions, if any one expression is valid, the script will result saying 'Valid age.' The OR operator is defined with a symbol, the double pipe that is ||.

Like AND operator, OR operator also has multiple options to write

1. Two expressions are written in different brackets, which are separated by a double pipe symbol.

    if [expression 1] || [expression 2]

2. Two expressions are in the same square bracket, and the symbol || is replaced by –o. Here is a single square bracket.

    if [expression 1 –o expression 2]

3. Two expressions are in the same double square bracket, and these are separated by double pipe symbol - ||.

    if [[expression 1 || expression 2]]

Now to define the OR operator in our script the 'if' script will look like below:

```
if [ $age -gt 18 ] || [ $age -lt 30 ]
```

The complete script will become like below:

```
#! /bin/bash

age=50
if [ $age -gt 18 ] || [ $age -lt 30 ]
then
        echo "Valid age."
else
        echo "Age not valid"
fi
```

Now, in this case, age 50 validates one expression, in that it is greater than 18, but the second expression is not valid as age is not less than 30. Since it meets one condition, when we execute the script, it should say 'Valid age.'

Let's execute the script now.

```
$ ./hello.sh
Valid age
```

This was expected.

Even if both conditions are met, the same result will happen.

Now let's create the situation where both expressions are false, and the script will execute the 'else' code. For that, we will change the expression of greater than (–gt) and less than (–lt) to equal to (-eq) in both expressions.

Now the script will become like below:

```
#! /bin/bash
```

```
age=50
if [ $age -eq 18 ] || [ $age -eq 30 ]
then
        echo "Valid age."
else
        echo "Age not valid"
fi
```
Let's execute the script now:
```
$ ./hello.sh
Age not valid
```

Since the ages 18 and 30, both are not equal to the value defined for variable 50; we got the output of code written in 'else' condition.

Next to understand the other way to write the OR operator with –o option or with double bracket. The two expressions will be separated using the double pipe symbol.

Let's see the script using a double pipeline:

```
#! /bin/bash

age=50
if [[ $age -eq 18 || $age -eq 30 ]]
then
        echo "Valid age."
else
        echo "Age not valid"
fi
```

When we execute the script, the same result of 'else' should come.

```
$ ./hello.sh
Age not valid
```

The output is correct.

Summary: In this chapter, you learned how to use AND and OR operator with the 'if' statement.

Three ways to use AND operator:

1. Both expressions in different square brackets and these brackets are separated by the symbol '&.'

2. Both expressions in the same square brackets and conditions are separated by –a

3. Two expressions are separated by double '&&' symbol, and all conditions are in between double square brackets.

Three ways to use OR operator:

1. Both expressions in different square brackets and these brackets are separated by the symbol '||.'

2. Both expressions in the same square brackets and conditions are separated by –o

3. Two expressions are separated by a double '||' symbol, and all conditions are in between double square brackets.

CHAPTER 9

Perform Arithmetic Operations

These are the operators used for any arithmetic or mathematic operations.

To understand it with a practical example, let's create two variable 'num1' with value 20 and the second variable as 'num2' with value 5. Now we want to do simple arithmetic operations like addition, subtraction, multiplication, division, and modulus.

Let's do this one by one.

To do addition, in front of the echo command, we write the two variables in double parentheses. There will be a space on both sides, and the '+' symbol separates both variables. The $ symbol has to be on the starting of the double parenthesis bracket. The script will be as below:

```
#! /bin/bash

num1=20
num2=5

echo $(( num1 + num2 ))
```

Now let's execute the script, the output should have the sum of two variables.

```
$ ./hello.sh
25
```

We got the output as 25, which results from the addition of 20 + 5. Means arithmetic operation has been performed on these two variables.

Similarly, you can do the other arithmetic operations in the same format. Below are the symbols used for the above mentioned operation:

Symbol	Operation
+	Addition
-	Subtraction
*	Multiplication
/	Division
%	Modulus

Modulus is an operation where, when we divide the two numbers, the number left as a remainder is the output.

Let's use the variables in our script with all arithmetic operations. The script will look like below:

```
#! /bin/bash

num1=20
num2=5

echo "addition of 20 + 5"
echo $(( num1 + num2 ))
echo "subtraction of 20 - 5"
echo $(( num1 - num2 ))
echo "multiplication of 20 * 5"
echo $(( num1 * num2 ))
echo "division of 20 / 5"
```

```
echo $(( num1 / num2 ))
echo "modulus of 20 % 5"
echo $(( num1 % num2 ))
```

Let's execute the script now.

```
$ ./hello.sh
addition of 20 + 5
25
subtraction of 20 - 5
15
multiplication of 20 * 5
100
Division of 20 / 5
4
modulus of 20 % 5
0
```

Now we can see all arithmetic operations have done well as expected results.

This is the way to perform simple arithmetic operations. There is another way to do these expressions by using 'expr.' To use 'expr' expression, the following changes will happen:

- In place of double parentheses, it will use a single parenthesis.

- In front of the variables, use the '$' symbol.

- For multiplication in place of the asterisk symbol (*), we will use it with a symbol backslash followed by an asterisk symbol - *.

To understand 'expr,' let's make the changes in our script. Also, changing the variable num1 and now the script will look as below:

```
#! /bin/bash

num1=21
num2=5

echo "addition of 21 + 5"
echo $( expr $num1 + $num2 )
echo "subtraction of 21 - 5"
echo $( expr $num1 - $num2 )
echo "multiplication of 21 * 5"
echo $( expr $num1 \* $num2 )
echo "division  of 21 / 5"
echo $( expr $num1 / $num2 )
echo "modulus of 21 % 5"
echo $( expr $num1 % $num2 )
```

Let's execute the script again. All operations should work, and now the change in modulus operations will be there.

```
$ ./hello.sh
addition of 21 + 5
26
subtraction of 21 - 5
16
multiplication of 21 * 5
105
Division of 21 / 5
4
modulus of 21 % 5
1
```

All looks good. Now you can see for modulus operation has an output as 1, which will be the remainder when 21 is divided by five as per arithmetic rules. Remember to use * for multiplication when 'expr' is being used.

Decimal Number

In this section, we will learn how to perform arithmetic operations with a decimal number. Default scripting does not support decimal arithmetic operations using the last two methods. To perform these operations, there are multiple tools available. We will use one tool. Before that, let's understand why the decimal number does not perform with the methods we have learned until now. To understand the problem, let's change the value of variable num1 from 21 to 20.5 and add both ways to the script.

Script will be as below:

```
#! /bin/bash

num1=20.5
num2=5

echo "addition of 20 + 5"
echo $(( num1 + num2 ))
echo "subtraction of 20 - 5"
echo $(( num1 - num2 ))
echo "multiplication of 20 * 5"
echo $(( num1 * num2 ))
echo "division of 20 / 5"
echo $(( num1 / num2 ))
echo "modulus of 20 % 5"
echo $(( num1 % num2 ))
echo " addition of 20.5 + 5"
echo $( expr $num1 + $num2 )
echo " subtraction of 20.5 - 5"
echo $( expr $num1 - $num2 )
echo " multiplication of 20.5 * 5"
echo $( expr $num1 \* $num2 )
echo " division of 20.5 / 5"
echo $( expr $num1 / $num2 )
echo " modulus of 20.5 % 5"
echo $( expr $num1 % $num2 )
```

Now let's execute the script. The output will be as below:

```
$ ./hello.sh
addition of 20 + 5
./hello.sh: line 7: 20.5: syntax error: invalid
arithmetic operator (error token is ".5")
subtraction of 20 - 5
./hello.sh: line 9: 20.5: syntax error: invalid
arithmetic operator (error token is ".5")
multiplication of 20 * 5
./hello.sh: line 11: 20.5: syntax error: invalid
arithmetic operator (error token is ".5")
division of 20 / 5
./hello.sh: line 13: 20.5: syntax error: invalid
arithmetic operator (error token is ".5")
 modulus of 20 % 5
./hello.sh: line 15: 20.5: syntax error: invalid
arithmetic operator (error token is ".5")
addition of 20.5 + 5
expr: non-integer argument
subtraction of 20.5 - 5
expr: non-integer argument
multiplication of 20.5 * 5
expr: non-integer argument
division of 20.5 / 5
expr: non-integer argument
modulus of 20.5 % 5
expr: non-integer argument
```

Here was can see with double parenthesis the error comes as "invalid arithmetic operator" and for operations using 'expr' gives the error "non-integer argument." To resolve such an issue, we can use tools, here in this book, we will explain a tool called 'bc' stands for basic calculator. Most Linux operating systems come along with 'bc' distribution. If this is not installed by default, it can be installed based on the Linux distribution you are working on (yum, yast, zypper, etc.). To learn in detail about bc, you can check the man page of bc as below.

```
man bc
```

This will open the man page of bc. With the definition of bc, you can see it defined as arbitrary-precision arithmetic language. It is a language for basic calculations. The man page will give all details for all options that can be used, but in this chapter, we will learn what we can do with bc for basic arithmetic operations.

To understand bc, we will use it in our script. Now we are keeping only the variables, and defining the decimal arithmetic operation, we use the echo command. With echo, write the numbers to be calculated with the symbol of operation in double-quotes, and after the quotes close, put a pipe symbol and write bc. This means the numbers written in double-quotes will be treated as input to the bc written on the right-hand side of the pipe symbol.

The script will become as below:

```
#! /bin/bash

num1=20.5
num2=5

echo "20.5+5" | bc
```

Let's execute the script.

```
$ ./hello.sh
25.5
```

It has given the right result for the two integers we have put across in the script.

Similarly, we can do other arithmetic operations using this command. In the below example, we are performing addition, subtraction, multiplication, division, and modulus for the same numbers:

```
#! /bin/bash

num1=20.5
num2=5

echo "addition of 20.5 + 5"
echo "20.5+5" | bc
echo "subtraction of 20.5 - 5"
echo "20.5-5" | bc
echo "multiplication of 20.5 * 5"
echo "20.5*5" | bc
echo "division of 20.5 / 5"
echo "20.5/5" | bc
echo "modulus of 20.5 % 5"
echo "20.5%5" | bc
```

Now let's execute the script.

```
$ ./hello.sh
addition of 20.5 + 5
25.5
subtraction of 20.5 - 5
15.5
multiplication of 20.5 * 5
102.5
division of 20.5 / 5
4
modulus of 20.5 % 5
.5
```

Now we can see all operations have worked and gave the right answers except division. For division, it has not given us the proper result. Let's understand why it happened and how to solve this problem.

To solve this problem with division, we will set a function of scale. The 'scale' defines up to which decimal place we want to see the result. In our example, let's define a scale for two decimal places, so we will give the value of scale as 2 in the division operation.

That can be done by writing 'scale' in the division command in the script.

```
echo "division  of 20.5 / 5"
echo "scale=2;20.5/5" | bc
```

If you want to see output up to 20 decimal places, you can write 20. For now, in our example, we are keeping the value as 2. Now we will execute the script.

```
$ ./hello.sh
addition of 20.5 + 5
25.5
subtraction of 20.5 - 5
15.5
multiplication of 20.5 * 5
102.5
division  of 20.5 / 5
4.10
modulus of 20.5 % 5
.5
```

That means that whenever we have to do a division operation, we need to define the up to which decimal place we want to see the output using the scale. If it is not written, then in output, it won't show any decimal number, which might be not the correct answer.

Also, in the above example, we have seen that we have used numbers for calculation and haven't used variables. The 'bc' works for variables too. Let's change the numbers to a variable in the same script and check

```
#! /bin/bash

num1=20.5
num2=5

echo "addition of 20.5 + 5"
echo "$num1+$num2" | bc
```

```
echo "subtraction of 20.5  - 5"
echo "$num1-$num2" | bc
```

Execute the script.

```
$ ./hello.sh
addition of 20.5 + 5
25.5
subtraction of 20.5  - 5
15.5
```

This looks fine.

As we have seen in the man page, 'bc' is not only for simple arithmetic calculations, but it can do much more than that. It can do arithmetic operations for square root, trigonometry, etc.

Square Root

Let's now find the square root of a number. This can be done by an option of bc known as 'sqrt.' Option 'sqrt' will help to find the square root of the number followed by this string. Also, like previous calculations, we used a simple 'bc' with no other options, but now for square root, we will use math operation; to get this done, we will add '-l option with bc. Flag '-l will call the math library in which there is a square root function.

For example, we want the square root of number 27. First, we will set the variable 'num' with 27. Also, we will set the scale to 2; as mentioned earlier, if you do not put the scale, there will be zero decimal places. After setting the scale, we will write 'sqrt' and, finally, the variable name. After writing this expression, we will pass this input to bc with option –l.

Script will be like below:

```
#! /bin/bash

num=27
echo "scale=2;sqrt($num)" | bc -l
Let's execute the script now.
$ ./hello.sh
5.19
```

We got the square root.

Arithmetic Power Function

Now let's learn the arithmetic power function. To get the power of any number, it is done by the caret symbol '^.' Here also we need to set the scale with the number of decimal places we want to see in the output. For this function also we will use the '-l' flag with 'bc.'

To understand with an example, now we want to get 2 to the power of 3, the script will become like below:

```
#! /bin/bash

num=4
echo "scale=2;2^3" | bc -l
```

Let's execute the script now.

```
$ ./hello.sh
8
```

Which looks good.

Some flags that can be used with 'bc' are listed below:

-h, --help	: Print the usage and exit.
-i, --interactive	: Force interactive mode.
-l, --mathlib	: Define the standard math library.

-w, --warn	: Give warnings for extensions to POSIX bc.
-s, --standard	: Process exactly the POSIX bc language.
-q, --quiet	: Do not print the normal GNU bc welcome.
-v, --version	: Print the version number and copyright and quit.

More operations that can be done with 'bc.'

++ var	: Post increment in variable

--var

++ var:

The variable is incremented by one, and the new value is the result of the expression.

-- var:

The variable is decremented by one, and the new value results from the expression.

var ++ :

The result of the expression is the value of the variable and then the variable is incremented by one.

var --

The result of the expression is the value of the variable, and then the variable is decremented by one.

There are many more functions like comparisons or logical operations as you can see in the man page dealing with bc.

Summary

We learned two ways of doing arithmetic operations:

1. Variables do arithmetic operations inside double parenthesis brackets.

2. Variables to do arithmetic operations inside single bracket using 'expr.' All are the same except multiplication for that * is used as a symbol to multiply.

3. To do simple arithmetic operations, we can use bc

4. The square root is done with the flag 'sqrt' along with bc and option '-l.'

5. To get power of any number, this is done with symbol '^.'

CHAPTER 10

The Case Statement

The case statement is a good alternate for multi-level if, then, or else statements, it helps to match several values again one value. Now let's see the basic syntax for the case statement.

```
#! /bin/bash

case expression in
    pattern1 )
        statement ;;
    pattern2 )
        statement ;;
    ...
esac
```

The first line is to start the case statement; we will start it with 'case,' and then 'expression' to evaluate; this can be any variable name or expression. This line ends with the keyword 'in.'

```
case expression in
```

The next lines will have multiple patterns. There could be multiple cases to evaluate. The pattern could be a string, a pattern, a regular expression. The pattern line is closed with the closing parenthesis, which means that this is the end of this case.

```
pattern1 )
```

After pattern comes the 'statement.' If the expression is true, then the 'statement' will be executed. At the end of the line, there will be double semicolon (;;), which means that the statement of the above case is ended and starts evaluating the next case. This will keep going as many cases we want to evaluate.

```
esac
```

The 'case' statement closes with 'esac', which is the reverse of case.

Let's understand how we can use the 'case' statement in practice with an example.

Let's say we are in the vehicle rental business. We will run an argument with a script, and we will save this argument in a variable. For the demo, we are keeping the variable name as 'vehicle.' The first value that will be entered into the argument is the value of the variable.

```
Variable=$1
```

To evaluate the variable 'vehicle' in the first expression after 'case', this variable will come here with a '$' sign. This variable will have the value that will be passed to the argument, may be a model, brand, etc. We will end this line with 'in.' The syntax will be as below:

```
case $vehicle in
```

Now comes the pattern; for now, we will just compare the pattern here. For example, if the variable 'vehicle' has the value 'car' in the argument, we will execute the statement. It will execute the statement as 'echo' that 'rent of the $vehicle is 100 dollars' and then end the line with two semicolon symbols (;;).

```
        "car" )
            echo "Rent of the $vehicle is 100 dollars"
;;
```

For the next pattern, let's say the argument given as 'van.' Now the variable value has become for 'van.' For this value, it will execute the echo statement with the message as "Rent of the $vehicle is 80 dollars," and again, the line will with ended with;;.

```
"van" )
        echo "Rent of the $vehicle is 80 dollars" ;;
```

Let's add two more patterns for the inputs 'bicycle' and 'truck', the same format will be used, and in echo, we can change the statement as required. In this way, we have now four patterns in this example.

```
"bicycle" )
         echo "Rent of the $vehicle is 5 dollars" ;;
         "truck" )
         echo "Rent of the $vehicle is 800 dollars" ;;
```

One more pattern we will add now that if the input is any other random value apart from these four patterns, then the pattern value will be '*.' In Linux '*' is a wild card, which means it matches everything. In that case, the statement will echo "vehicle unknown."

```
        * )
         echo "Unknown vehicle" ;;
```

Last, the script is ended by 'esac.'

The script will look as below:

```
#! /bin/bash

vehicale=$1
case $vehicle in
         "car" )
            echo "Rent of the $vehicle is 100 dollars" ;;
```

```
            "van" )
                 echo "Rent of the $vehicle is 80 dollars" ;;
            "bicycle" )
                 echo "Rent of the $vehicle is 5 dollars" ;;
            "truck" )
                 echo "Rent of the $vehicle is 500 dollars" ;;
            * )
                 echo "Unknown vehicle" ;;
esac
```

Now let's run our script. We will test it first, giving no argument. In this case, the condition * should execute

```
$ ./hello.sh
Unknown vehicle
```

This looks right. It has send an echo message of the default case.

Next, let's try with an argument car.

```
$ ./hello.sh car
Rent of the car is 100 dollars
```

In this case, the condition of the car is met as per the script, so the echo command for the car has executed and gives the right message as expected.

Similarly, we can test other patterns:

```
$ ./hello.sh van
Rent of the van is 80 dollars
$ ./hello.sh truck
Rent of the truck is 500 dollars
```

This way, we can check for the case strings, which are provided as input with the script. Right now, we are matching the strict pattern - that is matching the exact word which is given as an argument - but this could be any regular pattern also, that can also be done with the case. A regular pattern means an expression with strings of characters.

Now we will look another example of the case statement and then merge our knowledge with the previous example that we just read.

For now, we learned how 'case' works in scripting; we learned it with a basic syntax that we learned. Now in this example, we will evaluate some patterns in some cases.

Let's say we allow the user to enter any character, and then we evaluate that character. Based upon the character entered by the user, we will display if it is in uppercase, lowercase character, integer, any other special character, or that is not a character but a string. Now let's start writing our script.

First, after writing the script, we will define the script type that is the bash in our case. Next, we will ask to enter some character with an 'echo' command using the '-e' option. As already explained, the '-e' option to make script knows it must interpret the backslash escapes. We will use '\c' in the 'echo' string so that the user can provide input in the same line.

```
#! /bin/bash

echo -e "Enter some character : \c."
```

Now next, we will use the 'read' command to save that value in a variable. For this example, we keep that variable name as 'value'.

```
read    value
```

Any input entered by the user will not be stored in this variable. We will evaluate this value in the expression whether the entered character is an uppercase or lowercase. To check that, we will use patterns. There are rules to follow the pattern below is the list of some patterns.

- Small case: To evaluate if the pattern is lower case, small 'a-z' in square bracket [a-z] will be used.

- Upper case: To evaluate if the pattern is upper case, capital 'A-Z' in square bracket [A-Z] will be used.

- Integer: To evaluate if the pattern is an integer, '0-9' in square bracket [0-0] will be used.

- Special character: to evaluate if the pattern is a special character, '?' symbol will be used in without square bracket. The symbol question mark '?' is a pattern that expects any special one character letter. If there is one or more than one character, then the asterisk symbol '*' will be used. So, symbol '?' is for one character, and '*' is for one or more special characters in the string.

Let's now create our script

To evaluate the lower case character, it will be as below:

```
[a-z] )
    echo "User entered $value; it is a to z" ;;
```

To evaluate the upper case character, it will be as below:

```
[A-Z] )
    echo "User entered $value; it is A to Z" ;;
```

To evaluate the integer character, it will be as below:

```
[0-9] )
    echo "User entered $value, it is 0 to 9" ;;
```

To evaluate the single special character, it will be as below:

```
? )
    echo "User entered $value; it is a special character" ;;
```

To evaluate more than one special or mix characters, it will be as below:

```
* )
    echo "Unknown input" ;;
```

Now the script will become as below:

```
#! /bin/bash

echo -e "Enter some character : \c"
read value
case $value in
        [a-z] )
            echo "User entered $value; it is a to z" ;;
        [A-Z] )
            echo "User entered $value; it is A to Z" ;;
        [0-9] )
            echo "User entered $value, it is 0 to 9" ;;
        ? )
            echo "User entered $value, it is a special character" ;;
        * )
            echo "Unknown input" ;;
esac
```

Let's execute the script now:

- Giving input as 'f.'

```
$ ./hello.sh
Enter some character : f
User entered f; it is a to z
```

- Giving input as 'G.'

```
$ ./hello.sh
Enter some character : G
User entered G; it is a to z
```

Here we see an error. We have input as G., and when we gave input, the expected result was that the message should be "User entered G, it is A to Z, but it has come as small 'a to z'. That means it goes to the condition of the lower case. In case you also got the same error, then here a small hack to be done. The hack is you need to set system environmental LANG as C. The LANG environmental variable shows the language/locale and encoding, where C is the language setting. Run the below command on the prompt.

```
$ LANG=C
```

Now you have set the environment to the language C. This has to be done in case it does not meet the condition of uppercase. Let's try the script again with the same input as 'G.'

```
$ ./hello.sh
Enter some character : G
User entered G; it is A to Z
```

It worked well now.

- Giving input as '6.'

```
$ ./hello.sh
Enter some character : 6
User entered 6; it is 0 to 9
```

- Giving input as '%'

```
$ ./hello.sh
Enter some character : %
User entered % special character
```

- Giving input as '#sW4'

```
$ ./hello.sh
Enter some character : #sW4
Unknown input
```

This looks fine as expected from the rules defined in 'case.' In this way, you can match characters using the defined patterns. For more information, you can find a Wikipedia page on regular expressions. There will be more details about every symbol and character used in script.

So the 'case' is not just used for a strict letter or characters; you can evaluate any patterns.

Summary: In this chapter, we learned the 'case' statement for simple arguments with script and using the pattern. We learned its syntax and some options that are used generally in scripting.

CHAPTER 11

Array Variables

We have learned so far about variables. Variables in shell scripting can hold a single value. Now think of a situation where we have a large number of values to hold; in that case, it will be a complex situation to create a variable for each value. The array comes into the picture now. The array can hold multiple values at the same time. It has a mechanism of grouping the variables.

How to use an array? It is simple, define the name of an array like a variable. For example, we will keep 'os' as the name of the variable. To declare the values, the 'os' will be followed by 'equal to' symbol (=), and in parentheses, there will be names of elements declared. A space will separate the element names that will be in individual parentheses. In this example, we gave three elements of the array variables 'os' as Ubuntu, windows, and kali.

It shows the following:

```
os=('ubuntu' 'windows' 'kali')
```

To display the value, it can be done with 'echo' command as - "${os[@]}." The symbol '@' will show all the elements of the array variable 'os.'

Script will look as below:

```
#! /bin/bash

os=('ubuntu' 'windows' 'kali')
echo "${os[@]}"
```

Let's execute the script now.

```
$ ./hello.sh
ubuntu windows kali
```

This way, in output, we can see all element values.

All the values in the curly bracket have their index numbers, starting from number 0. In the above example, there are three elements defined: Ubuntu, windows, and kali. Since the index number starts from 0, that means they have 0,1 and 2 index numbers assigned in serial order. To print any specific element, we can use these index numbers.

To display only 'windows' in output, in the 'echo' command inside the square bracket we will define the index number as 1, as shown below in the script

```
#! /bin/bash

os=('ubuntu' 'windows' 'kali')

echo "${os[@]}"
echo "${os[1]}"
```

When we execute the script, two lines will be the output; for the line with '[@]', it should display all elements, and the next line with '[1]' should show only index number 1 that is 'windows.'

```
$ ./hello.sh
ubuntu windows kali
windows
```

80

This looks perfect.

Next, let's look how to print the indexes of the array that can be done by adding an exclamation mark symbol (!) before the variable name in brackets "${!os[@]}". Now we will add this also in the script.

```
#! /bin/bash

os=('ubuntu' 'windows' 'kali')

echo "${os[@]}"
echo "${os[1]}"
echo "${!os[@]}"
```

We will execute the script now

```
$ ./hello.sh
ubuntu windows kali
windows
0 1 2
```

Now we can see the index numbers of the array. Since we have three elements, it has shown 0,1, and 2.

Next, let's see how to print the length of the array, that can be done by adding hash symbol (#) before the variable name 'os' as "${#os[@]}." Let's add this line also in the script:

```
#! /bin/bash

os=('ubuntu' 'windows' 'kali')

echo "${os[@]}"
echo "${os[1]}"
echo "${!os[@]}"
echo "${#os[@]}"
```

Now we will execute the script

```
$ ./hello.sh
ubuntu windows kali
windows
0 1 2
3
```

Since we have three elements, we have the number 3, which is the length of the array.

There will be situations when you need to add elements to the array. How to do that? It needs to add a line for the same array variable name. Here variable name is 'os' and then with 'os' add a square bracket having the index number you want and followed by the value you want to add, in this example it is 'mac.' The following line will add it

```
os[3]='mac'
```

Now, after adding this, the script will look as below:

```
#! /bin/bash

os=('ubuntu' 'windows' 'kali')
os[3]='mac'
echo "${os[@]}"
echo "${os[1]}"
echo "${!os[@]}"
echo "${#os[@]}"
```

Now let's execute the script:

```
$ ./hello.sh
ubuntu windows kali mac
windows
0 1 2 3
4
```

We can see at index number 3; a new 4th element, 'mac', has been added to the array.

If we want to update an existing element, that can also be done in the same way by writing the number of index numbers and the value of the element. If on the same index number already there is an element, this new value will replace it. In the example, let's change the index number 0 from 'ubuntu' to 'mac.' The script will be as below now:

```
os=('ubuntu' 'windows' 'kali')
os[0]='mac'
echo "${os[@]}"
echo "${os[1]}"
echo "${!os[@]}"
echo "${#os[@]}"
```

Let's execute the script now.

```
$ ./hello.sh
mac windows kali
windows
0 1 2
3
```

Now we can see 'mac' is at element '0' now. So, if you want to define any element at a certain index number that can be done by using this method.

Next, we will see how to remove an element from an array. 'unset can do this' and the name of the array. In our case, it is 'os.' With 'os' we will add a square bracket having the element number to be removed as shown below:

```
unset os[2]
```

He has an added number 2. That means element at number 2 will be removed when we will execute the script. Now the script will be as below:

```
#! /bin/bash

os=('ubuntu' 'windows' 'kali')
unset os[2]
os[3]='mac'
echo "${os[@]}"
echo "${os[1]}"
echo "${!os[@]}"
echo "${#os[@]}"
```

Now let's execute the script. At index number 2, 'kali' is there, so that should be removed.

```
$ ./hello.sh
ubuntu windows mac
windows
0 1 3
3
```

We can see 'kali' is not in output now.

As we have removed index 2, then why has 'mac' has come to its place? It happens like this; in scripting, we can add an element at any index, but the output will print in sequence; there will be no blank space. For example, for 'mac' we will change the element number to 6, still when we will execute the result will display the same.

Now the script will be as below:

```
#! /bin/bash

os=('ubuntu' 'windows' 'kali')
unset os[2]
os[6]='mac'
echo "${os[@]}"
```

84

```
echo "${os[1]}"
echo "${!os[@]}"
echo "${#os[@]}"
```

Now we will execute the script.

```
$ ./hello.sh
ubuntu windows mac
windows
0 1 6
3
```

Here we can see that the null position is ignored, and there are no gaps in the output. That means some members of the array are not initialized, and gaps in the array are acceptable.

Scripting in Linux permits arrays operation on variables as well. Even if the variables are not explicitly declared as an array. Let's understand this with an example in our existing script. We will add a new variable 'string', and we assign any random value to it. We will add the 'echo' command to display all elements of this variable.

The script will look as below:

```
#! /bin/bash

os=('ubuntu' 'windows' 'kali')
unset os[2]
os[6]='mac'
echo "${os[@]}"
echo "${os[1]}"
echo "${!os[@]}"
echo "${#os[@]}"
string=abcdefghi
echo "${string[@]}"
```

Now we will execute the script

```
$ ./hello.sh
```

```
ubuntu windows mac
windows
0 1 6
3
abcdefghi
```

Here we can see that the script has taken string value as an array and print it will the array rules. That means that it can also use this notation.

Now let's print the 0th element of the array; to do this, we will add a line to print on 0th element by putting the value as 0 for 'echo' command.

```
#! /bin/bash

os=('ubuntu' 'windows' 'kali')
unset os[2]
os[6]='mac'
echo "${os[@]}"
echo "${os[1]}"
echo "${!os[@]}"
echo "${#os[@]}"
string=abcdefghi
echo "${string[@]}"
echo "${string[0]}"
```

Now we will execute the script

```
$ ./hello.sh
ubuntu windows mac
windows
0 1 6
3
Abcdefghi
abcdefghi
```

Here we can see in the output of the 0th element is same. That means it does the indexing in the same way as the array does when it has multiple elements. Here we consider the whole string as a single element.

If we try to print index number 1, then what will happen, let's check in the script. We will add a line to print the index value as 1. The script will become as below:

```
#! /bin/bash

os=('ubuntu' 'windows' 'kali')
unset os[2]
os[6]='mac'
echo "${os[@]}"
echo "${os[1]}"
echo "${!os[@]}"
echo "${#os[@]}"

string=abcdefghi
echo "${string[@]}"
echo "${string[0]}"
echo "${string[1]}"
```

Executing the script now.

```
$ ./hello.sh
ubuntu windows mac
windows
0 1 6
3
abcdefghi
abcdefghi

$
```

Here we can see there is nothing but a blank line that has come at the place of printing element 1. Why did this happen? This has happened as we treat a string as a variable value in an array; the array value at the zeroth index will be the string. Even if we print the number of elements in the array, it will come out as 1. Let's check this also to verify how many elements we have in the array.

```bash
#! /bin/bash

os=('ubuntu' 'windows' 'kali')
unset os[2]
os[6]='mac'
echo "${os[@]}"
echo "${os[1]}"
echo "${!os[@]}"
echo "${#os[@]}"

string=abcdefghi
echo "${string[@]}"
echo "${string[0]}"
echo "${string[1]}"
echo "${#string[@]}"
```

Let's execute the script now:

```
$ ./hello.sh
ubuntu windows mac
windows
0 1 6
3
abcdefghi
abcdefghi
1
```

Here we can see in the output for the whole string that it counted one element in the array. And it number 1 element by default as the 0th element on the array.

Summary:

In this chapter, we learned:

How to define an array and elements and print all the values or individual values

How to get the index numbers of the array

How to get a total number of elements in an array

How to print a new value of the defined element by overwriting the element value.

How to remove an element from an array

We also count strings as a single element of an array.

CHAPTER 12

WHILE Loops

In this chapter, we will understand loops and how to use it. First, let's understand what loops are. The loops are used to execute the list of commands repeatedly. The place where the repeated command to use, that is where we can use loops.

Before we begin, let's understand the syntax of the loop.

The keyword for loop is 'while', which will start the loop command with a square bracket we can give the condition which needs to evaluate.

```
While [ condition ]
```

If the condition is true, it will move to the section 'do', which contains the list of commands to be executed. Once commands are done, and it completes the while loop. It ends with 'done.'

```
do
   command1
   command2
   command3
done
```

So the complete syntax will be as below

```
while [ condition ]
```

```
do
   command1
   command2
   command3
done
```

Let's understand it more with an example.

We want to print the numbers 1 to 10 using the 'while' loop. So first let's declare a variable 'n' as value 1

```
n=1
```

Now let's put a condition in 'while' statement to check if the value of 'n' is less than or equal to 10 or not. We will use the '–le' flag. We have learned the 'le' flag in 'if' condition. It is to compare the number is 'less than or equal to' value. So the syntax will become as below:

```
while [ $n -le 10 ]
```

Next, between 'do and 'done', we can execute any command. We will use 'echo' command to print the value 'n', but we are not done only with this, as this will only print the value of 'n', which is 1. It will execute infinitely because one is always less than 10, which is a true condition, which will make a loop to keep repeating it. So we need a code to increment the value on variable 'n' by one it executes every time, and then we are good to go. That can be done by adding a line having command executing n+1, as shown below, in the example. This will keep on adding 1 to the value of variable every time it executes, and once its value becomes equal to or greater than 10, it will end the loop.

```
do
   echo "$n"
   n=(( $n+1 ))
done
```

So the script will become as below:

```
#! /bin/bash

#   while loops
n=1
while [ $n -le 10 ]
do
        echo "$n"
        n=$(( n+1 ))
done
```

Let's execute the script now

```
$ ./hello.sh
1
2
3
4
5
6
7
8
9
10
```

It prints value from 1 to 10, now let's understand what is happening in this loop. Initially, we assigned the value of 'n' as 1. When it reach to 'while' loop, this loop evaluates if the value of n is less than or equal to 10. First, the value of n was one as the defined value of the variable, which is less than or equal to 10. This is a true condition, so it prints the value of $n as 1. Next, with n+1, it increment the value of 1, now the value of n becomes 2. Once again, it goes in loop to 'while' condition with the value of n as 2, which is still less than or equal to 10, so once again, echo "$n" code is executed, and it prints the number 2. In this way, it will keep increment the number by one every time until it reached the value of n as 10. Once it reached value 10, still the condition is valid as ten is now equal to 10. Once the value of n becomes 11, and it reached to 'while' condition, now 11 is not less than or equal to 10; this makes the loop condition false, and commands written in 'do' will not be executed, and it will end the loop by done.

The increment of the variable can be done in several ways. In the above example, we have seen one format.

n=$((n+1)), other way to use just ((n++))to increment the value of n, which means post-increment. If we use this way, the script will become as below:

```
#! /bin/bash

#   while loops
n=1
while [ $n -le 10 ]
do
        echo "$n"
        (( n++ ))
Done
```

If we execute the script, the result will be the same as above. Another way is to use way pre-increment, that is done as ((++n)), the script will look as below:

```
#! /bin/bash

#   while loops
n=1
while [ $n -le 10 ]
do
        echo "$n"
        (( ++n ))
Done
```

If you execute, the result will still be the same.

Another way to use a while statement is to use double parentheses instead of using square brackets. In that case, '-le' will be replaced by symbol '<=' as we have used in 'if' statement. When we use this way, the script will look as below:

```
#! /bin/bash

#   while loops
n=1
while (( $n <= 10 ))
do
        echo "$n"
        (( ++n ))
Done
```

When this script is executed, the result would be the same. It will still print the value 1 to 10.

Using Sleep with Loop

To proceed further, we will use the below script, and when we execute this, it prints the numbers 1 to 10.

```
#! /bin/bash

#   while loops
n=1
while [ $n -le 10 ]
do
        echo "$n"
        (( n++ ))
Done
```

When we execute the script, all values from 1 to 10 are written as a flash on the screen. Let's say we want some delay while printing the values; we can do this with 'sleep' command. After 'sleep' we can give any number. The number we give will make the loop to pause for that many seconds. For our example, we are using 'sleep' value as 1. Means after every increment of the variable by 1, the loop will pause for 1 second and then proceed. The script will look as below now:

```
#! /bin/bash

#   while loops
n=1
while [ $n -le 10 ]
do
        echo "$n"
        (( n++ ))
        sleep 1
done
```

This time when we will execute the script, after every line, it will pause for a second. In this book, we will show the output that will be the same, but when you execute on the terminal, you can experience the pause of 1 second after every line until loops end.

```
$ ./hello.sh
1  ← pause 1 second
2  ← pause 1 second
3  ← pause 1 second
4  ← pause 1 second
5  ← pause 1 second
6  ← pause 1 second
7  ← pause 1 second
8  ← pause 1 second
9  ← pause 1 second
10 ← pause 1 second
$
```

Now we saw there was a pause of 1 second after every line, and once the condition is met, it comes out of the loop, and you can see the prompt on the terminal.

No increment

What will happen if there is no increment for the variable means we will remove the command to increment the variable by 1? If we do that, then the loop will keep running infinitely. Let's do the change and see how the script looks:

```
$ vi hello.sh
#! /bin/bash

#   while loops
n=1

while [ $n -le 10 ]
do
        echo "$n"
        sleep 1
done
```

Here we have removed line - ((n++)), Now let's execute the script. Since there will be no increment, so the loop will keep on running. To end the script, we can use ctrl+c to end the loop and get back the prompt on the terminal.

```
$ ./hello.sh
1
1
1
1
1
^C
$
```

So if you ever want a continuous loop, you give the condition, which is always true. Also, when you have a loop which is having a true condition with no sleep parameter, then it will execute infinitely. This can cause performance degradation of your computer

Open Multiple Terminals with Loop

Using a loop, it can open multiple terminals. To do this function, you must be aware which kind of terminal can run on your system.

Now let's open three terminals using the loop. Then in 'while', we will set the value as 3, so the loop will keep opening terminals until this number is reached. We want to open the terminal using our script, so we need to define what kind of terminal we want to open. In Linux, mostly xterm and gnome are there. Depending on your operating system, you can select that terminal type. For this example, let's open the gnome terminal. We will add a line to open the terminal as below in the 'do' section is 'gnome-terminal &.' Now the script will be as below:

```
#! /bin/bash

#   while loops
n=1

while [ $n -le 3 ]
do
        echo "$n"
        (( n++ ))
        gnome-terminal &
done
```

to open xterm terminal, the script will be as below:

```
#! /bin/bash

#   while loops
n=1
while [ $n -le 3 ]
do
        echo "$n"
        (( n++ ))
        xterm &
done
```

When you execute the above scripts, the terminal mentioned in the scripts, three terminals will open.

Read Files using WHILE Loop

In this section, we will learn how to read files using a loop. There are multiple ways of reading files using while loop; we will use some of them in this book.

The first way of reading files using 'while' loop is using input redirection. Add 'read' command after 'while' and then write a variable in which we will save the content of the file line by line. For this example, we will keep the variable as 'p'.

```
while read p
```

Next, in the 'do' section, we need to write commands. We will do echo to the variable with $p.

```
do
        echo $p
```

Next step, we need to read the file. We will use function file redirection to read the file using an angular bracket symbol (< or >). This is a common Linux functionality to redirect the input from or to a file. The direction towards which the angular bracket is pointing to will take the input from the file on the open side of the bracket.

For the script, with 'done', we will use an angular bracket to get input format file we want to read. In this example, we will read our script file, hello.sh.

```
done < hello.sh
```

When the script executes, the above line will read the file hello.sh, and this will go to variable 'p' as a value in 'while', then 'echo' will print the line that it will read from the variable. In this way, the content of hello.sh will go in while loop.

The script will look as below:

```
#! /bin/bash

#   while loops
while read p
do
    echo $p
done < hello.sh
```

Let's execute the script now

```
$ ./hello.sh
#! /bin/bash

# while loops
while read p
do
echo $p
done < hello.sh

$
```

You can see that the script has printed the content of the file.

The other way to read the file in a single variable and then print it. If you know pipe (|) function in Linux, it will be easier to understand.

We will make some changes in our script; we will add a 'cat' command before 'while' to read a file and then the filename to read that it is hello.sh. After that, on the same line, we will keep 'while' will 'read p'. What will happen now, whatever the content is read by 'cat' command, will become the input for the while command. The output of the 'cat' will be the input to the 'while' loop, and then it will read it using the 'read' command and finally with 'echo' will print the content of the file.

Now the script will be as below:

```
#! /bin/bash

#   while loops
cat hello.sh | while read p
do
    echo $p
done
```

We will execute the script now.

```
$ ./hello.sh
#! /bin/bash

# while loops
cat hello.sh | while read p
do
echo $p
done
$
```

You can see the content of the file is printed as before.

While with IFS

Until now, we have learned two methods; the first way is using the input redirection, and we read the second way is the file content into one variable and then print it. Sometimes it is hard to read a file using these two methods because of special characters in the file, for example, line indentation. So what we can do is, in the second method, we will use the read command once again, but we will use the Internal Field Separator (IFS). The script uses IFS to determine how to work splitting that is how to recognize word boundaries. Let's see how to do it with IFS.

In our example, we will use 'while' keyword here and after 'while' use IFS followed by equal to sign (=) with space. It is important to know that we are not assigning the 'read' to IFS, we are assigning a space to IFS. This is important to keep a space between the '=' sign and the 'read' command. With the 'read' command, we will use '-r' flag here. The flag '-r' prevents that backslash-escape from being interpreted. If we don't use this, backslash can be interpreted in an unknown way and may cause wrong output.

```
while IFS= read line
```

For this example, we are using a variable name in 'read' command as 'line,' which is more meaningful, and we will use the input redirection method to provide the input file hello.sh with 'done'.

```
do
    echo $line
done < hello.sh
```

Now the script will be as below:

```
#! /bin/bash

#   while loops
while IFS= read line
do
    echo $line
done < hello.sh
```

We will execute the script now:

```
$ ./hello.sh
#! /bin/bash

# while loops
while IFS= read line
do
echo $line
done < hello.sh
$
```

The output is the same as expected.

There is another option to use IFS, that is before read command, in place of space given, we can also put a set of single quotes with space in between. As below

```
while IFS=' ' read line
```

Even if we use this and execute the script, the output will be the same.

Using 'while' with a File Path

We want to read a file which is not in the current working directory but in some other folder. Now let's understand how can we do that.

In our example, we will read file /etc/vconsole.conf using the 'while' loop. Before we proceed, let's read the content of /etc/vconsole.conf file using the 'cat' command.

```
$ cat vconsole.conf
KEYMAP=us
FONT=eurlatgr.psfu
FONT_MAP=
FONT_UNIMAP=
```

We do only one change in our script to define the path of the file as an input file to read. We will replace hello.sh with /etc/vconsole.conf as below:

```
done < /etc/vconsole.conf
```

After this change, the script will look as below:

```
#! /bin/bash

#  while loops
while IFS= read -r line
do
```

```
    echo $line
done < /etc/vconsole.conf
```

We will execute the script now

```
$ ./hello.sh
KEYMAP=us
FONT=eurlatgr.psfu
FONT_MAP=
FONT_UNIMAP=
$
```

The content is the same as the file we have read before.

There are more methods to read the file using file descriptors. That we will learn in coming chapters.

Summary:

We learned the while loop, its function, and syntax.

We also learned different ways to increment the value of a variable.

We understood how to use sleep in a loop, how to open multiple terminals using a loop, multiple ways to read the file with a loop using the angular bracket, pipe symbol, and using IFS in two ways, with space and ' '.

By defining the path of file also the while loop can read the contents of the file.

CHAPTER 13

UNITL Loops

Now we will learn about the 'until' loop. Until loop is similar to 'while' loop with a slight difference. The difference 'while' and 'until' is, like in while the command defined between do and done executes if the condition is true, but in 'until' the commands will execute if the condition is false.

Before we proceed, let's understand the syntax of 'until' loop.

With the keyword 'until' in square brackets or double parenthesis we write the condition

```
until [ condition] or until (( condition ))
```

If the condition is false, the commands written between 'do' and 'done' will be executed.

The complete syntax will be as below:

```
 until [ condition]
do
         command1
         command2
         …..
         …..
         command
done
```

The listed commands will execute only if the condition is false, that is the difference between 'while' and 'until' loop.

Let's understand this with an example.

Once again, we want to print the value from 1 to 10 on the terminal; we will create a variable 'n' and assign value 1 to it.

```
n=1
```

Next, we will update the 'condition' in 'until' statement. This time for variable $n, we will assign flag as '-ge'. We have learned before about '-ge' that is greater than and equal to in if' and next to it there is number 10. Now the condition becomes, if the value of n is not greater than or equal to 10, it will execute the commands under 'do.'

```
until [ $n -ge 10 ]
```

In this case, we want to print the value of n by the 'echo $n' command. To increment the number, we can write notation n+1 in double parentheses.

```
do
    echo $n
    (( n+1 ))
done
```

The complete script will become as below:

```
$ vi hello.sh
#! /bin/bash

#   until loops
n=1
until [ $n -ge 10 ]
do
    echo $n
    n=$(( n+1 ))
done
```

Let's execute the script now:

```
$ ./hello.sh
1
2
3
4
5
6
7
8
9
```

It has a printed value of 1 to 9. Why is it happening here? This has happened; the condition '$n –ge 10' is false. When we started our script with n=1. In the 'until' condition, it checked if one is greater than or equal to 10, and it checks for the false condition. The 'until' loop works when the condition is false, which makes commands to execute under 'do.' Under 'do' there are two commands, first is to print the value of n and next is to increment the value of n by 1. It keeps repeating in a loop until it reaches number 11. Once it reaches 11, the condition becomes true, and the loop will not execute further.

To print 10 in the output, then in a condition of 'until' we will replace –ge with –gt. Means now the condition will become true once n reaches to 10; this makes the condition true, and the loop will end.

Like the 'while' loop, in the 'until' loop the square brackets in the 'condition' can be replaced by double parenthesis and the flag –gt will be replaced by angular bracket '>'. Let's make these changes and run the script. Since this time, we apply the condition only 'greater than' and removed 'equal to', so now it will print the number 10 also.

```
#! /bin/bash

#   until loops

n=1

until (( $n > 10 ))
do
    echo $n
    n=$(( n+1 ))
done
```

Let's execute the script

```
$ ./hello.sh
1
2
3
4
5
6
7
8
9
10
```

We can see the output ten is printed now.

As we have seen in 'while' there are multiple ways to increment the variable. Let's see the same here as well.

We can replace n+1 to n++ or ++n; all these methods will do the increment by 1 to variable n at every step. Let's try one of these, and we will see the result is the same. On more change we have done, we have used symbols for greater than or equal to (>=) in the 'until' condition.

The script will be as below:

```
#! /bin/bash

#   until loops
n=1
until (( $n >= 10 ))
do
    echo $n
    n=$(( ++n ))
done
```

We will execute the script now:

```
$ ./hello.sh
1
2
3
4
5
6
7
8
9
```

We can see the result is the same.

CHAPTER 14

FOR Loops

Now let's learn how to use 'for' loops in shell scripting. The 'for' loops are also used to loop over the list of values and execute the commands in the loop.

First, let's understand the syntax of 'for' loop

There are multiple syntaxes of 'for' loop; we will show a few of them.

Method 1

```
for VARIABLE in 1 2 3 4 5 .. N
do
    command1
    command2
    commandN
done
```

In this method, first, we use the 'for' keyword and declare the key, 'VARIABLE' followed by a keyword 'in' and then we gave a list of values, for example, 1 2 3 4 5 ..N or it could be in the list format. The list format we will learn later in the chapter when we will see the examples.

Method 2

```
for VARIABLE in file1 file2 file3
do
    command1
    command2
    commandN
done
```

You can give the files as an input here. All the commands will be between 'do' and 'done' which will be executed

Method 3

```
for OUTPUT in $(Linux command here)
do
    command1
    command2
    commandN
done
```

You can give Linux command using the syntax as shown above. We can assign this command as a variable.

Method 4

```
for (( EXP1; EXP2; EXP3 ))
do
    command1
    command2
    commandN
done
```

The 'for' loop can also be used similarly as in C programming. In this method, we can use a three number of expressions between double parentheses. We can use the first expression to initialize the value, second is to compare, or if it fulfills the condition, the third expression is where we can increment the value of the first expression.

Let's now understand the 'for' loop in a better way. We will start by using method 1.

Let's say we want to read some numbers and then print them. In our example, we will use five numbers. Also, we will set the variable name as 'v'.

```
for v 1 2 3 4 5
```

Between 'do' and 'done' keyword, we will write the commands to execute. In 'do', we will run command 'echo' to the numbers using the variable 'v'.

```
do
    echo $v
done
```

So the complete script will be as below:

```
#! /bin/bash

#   for loops
for v in 1 2 3 4 5
do
   echo $v
done
```

Let's execute the script now:

```
$ ./hello.sh
1
2
3
4
5
```

It has printed numbers 1 to 5; it is quite simple. Now consider a scenario we have hundreds of numbers to be printed, then we might not use this method. For that, we will change this syntax. In that case, we will give a range in curly brackets. A double dot symbol separates the range of numbers. The script will now be as shown below

```
#! /bin/bash

#   for loops
for v in {1..10}
do
   echo $v
done
```

Let's execute the script.

```
$ ./hello.sh
1
2
3
4
5
6
7
8
9
10
$
```

It prints all range numbers.

There is one more way of using the range. In the previous example, 1 was the starting value, 10 was the ending value, and we separated these two by putting two dots. If after 10, we add two more dots and give a number, this number will be the increment number. The format will be as below:

```
{START..END..INCREMENT}
```

For example, after 10 two more dots added, followed by number 2. Means we want to increment the value by two like this: {1..10..2}.

Now every time the loop executes, the variable value will keep increasing by 2.

The script will look as below:

```
#! /bin/bash

#   for loops
for v in {1..10..2}
do
   echo $v
done
Let's execute the script now.
$ ./hello.sh
1
3
5
7
9
$
```

Here we can see, 1 starts the number, and every time it goes through a 'for' loop, the value gets incremented by 2.

Some old scripts do not follow this format, so you need to check if your script version supports this format. Now here the question may come, how to check the version, this can be done by checking the first system variable for which shell you are working on, and then check the version of the shell. It is shown below:

```
$ echo $SHELL
/bin/bash
$ echo $BASH_VERSION
4.4.23(1)-release
```

Here we can see the system is running bash shell (/bin/bash) ver 4.4.23(1)-release. For bash, it does not work on below version 3.

Method

Let's see another method for loop command by using three expressions between the double parentheses. In the first expression, we will use variable 'v' with value 0. In the next expression, we will check if the variable value is less than five or not and, in third expression, we will increment the value of the variable by 1. All three expressions are separated by a single semicolon (;).

```
for v in (( v=1; v<5; v++ ))
```

Between 'do' and 'done' we will display the value of variable v, until the loop ends.

The script will be as below now:

```
#! /bin/bash

#   for loops
for (( v=0; v<5; v++ ))
do
   echo $v
done
```

Let's execute the script now.

```
$ ./hello.sh
0
1
2
3
4
```

Here we can see the value printed by script is from 0 to 5. Since the condition is that it should print the value less than 5, so after 4, the loop ends.

Loop 'for' with Files and Commands

Now let's see how to use 'for' loop with some command with some example for better understanding.

In this way, we write command with 'for' expression, which will be the variable in this case. After command, we provide keyword 'in' followed by which we give some input in the form of some list or some commands. Then between do and done keyword, we give the command to execute the variable value. The basic syntax will be as below:

```
for command in
do
     echo $command
done
```

We can give a list of commands to execute. Let's understand with an example. In the 'for' expression, we will give a list of commands, which are ls, pwd, and date. These commands will be executed one by one in order by which we write the commands. Between 'do' and 'done', we will write echo to mark a line with variable name, so this will give information about which command is getting executed now. Next to this line, we will show the output of the command by displaying the value of $command. The script will look as below:

```
#! /bin/bash

#   for loops
for command in ls pwd date
do
   echo "---------- $command ----------"
   $command
done
```

Let's execute the script now.

```
$ ./hello.sh
```

```
---------- ls ------------
backup   doc   examples   glass   hello.sh   hello.sh.org
myhome   scripts   test
---------- pwd -----------
/home/user1
---------- date ----------
Fri Nov 15 16:31:39 IST 2019
$
```

In this way, we can give as many numbers of commands to be executed one by one, and it can print the output as explained in the above example.

Let's take one practical example.

We are in our home directory right now, and we want to print all the directories in it. First, let's list our home folder, and then see the list of files and directories

```
$ ls -l
total 32
drwxr-xr-x 2 user1 users       6 Nov 15 16:35 backup
-rw-r--r-- 1 user1 users     454 Nov 15 16:37 doc
-rw-r--r-- 1 user1 users     501 Nov 15 16:38 examples
-rw-r--r-- 1 user1 users       0 Nov 15 16:38 glass
-rwxr-xr-x 1 user1 users     115 Nov 15 16:28 hello.sh
-rwxr-xr-x 1 user1 users     357 Nov 11 22:15 hello.sh.org
drwxr-xr-x 2 user1 users       6 Nov 15 16:34 myhome
drwxr-xr-x 2 user1 users       6 Nov 15 17:19 qrt
function is the
-rw-r--r-- 1 user1 users   13336 Nov 15 16:39 scripts
drwxr-xr-x 2 user1 users       6 Nov 15 16:34 test
$
```

First, in our script, we will define a variable 'item' for 'for' expression. To display the content of our home directory, in 'for' expression we will fill the commands with an asterisk sign *.

```
for item in *
```

Between 'do' and 'done', we will use 'if' statement. In the 'if' statement, we will evaluate the value of variable ''item' weather that is a directory or not; if that is a directory, the script should print it. We can do this by adding a flag '-d' and the variable 'item'. As a format of 'if' expression, there is 'then' and 'else' sections. When the statement is true, it goes to the 'then' section. In 'then' we will 'echo' the directory name. Lastly, the if statement will be close by 'fi'.

```
if [ -d $item ]
then
    echo $item
fi
```

The script will become as below:

```
#! /bin/bash

#   for loops
for item in *
do
  if [ -d $item ]
  then
    echo $item
    fi
done
```

Let's execute the script now.

```
$ ./hello.sh
backup
myhome
./hello.sh: line 7: [: too many arguments
test
$
```

We can see it has displayed all directories names in the current directory. Apart from that, there is an error also:

```
./hello.sh: line 7: [: too many arguments
```

Why has it come? This error has come for a directory shown below:

```
drwxr-xr-x 2 user1 users      6 Nov 15 17:19 qrt function is the
```

In this directory, there are four keyword functions - qrt, function, is and the. Space separates these four keyword functions. Because of this, the script cannot understand if these are the separate names of a single name of a directory. Let's delete this directory and then rerun the script. The error should not come.

```
$ rm -rv "qrt function is the"
removed directory 'qrt function is the'
$ ./hello.sh
backup
myhome
test
$
```

It has worked perfectly by printing all the directories.

To print all the files in the script, we will change the flag '-d' to '-f'. Let's do this change and print all the files.

```
 #! /bin/bash

# for loops
for item in *
do
  if [ -f $item ]
  then
    echo $item
   fi
done
```

Let's execute the script.

```
$ ./hello.sh
doc
examples
glass
hello.sh
hello.sh.org
scripts
$
```

It has printed all the files now.

Understood 'for' loop and the three syntax methods. Loop 'for' with files and commands.

CHAPTER 15

SELECT Loops

In this chapter, we will learn about 'select' loops.

First, let's understand why we use loops. 'Select' allows us to construct easy menus. Whenever you write a script that requires menus, there we can use 'select' loop.

Before we process, first, let's understand the basic syntax of the loop.

```
#! /bin/bash

select varName in list
do
    command1
    command2
    ....
    .....
    commandN
done
```

This loop starts by defining 'select' then the variable name. Next will be the keyword 'in' and in last, will have a list of items. Then between 'do' and 'done' keywords, there will be a list of commands that will be executed based on the list you have provided. Let's learn this in detail now.

We will start the 'select' loop and keep variable labeling as 'name' followed by the keyword 'in'. In the list, we will give some names.

```
select name in mark john tom ben
```

Between 'do' and 'done', we will write command to print the name with 'echo' and the variable name. After a variable name, we will add a keyword as 'selected'.

```
do
   echo "$name selected."
done
```

The script will look as below:

```
#! /bin/bash

select name in mark john tom ben
do
   echo "$name selected."
done
```

Let's execute the script.

```
$ ./hello.sh
1) mark
2) john
3) tom
4) ben
#?
```

Here you can see the list of names that are listed in a line. It associates every name with a number. Now the script is waiting for us to input any of the numbers in the list from 1 to 4. For now, we are giving number 2, which is associated with 'john' and let's see what happens

```
$ ./hello.sh
1) mark
2) john
```

```
3) tom
4) ben
#? 2
john selected
#?
```

Here we can see that as we entered number 2, it displays the name 'john'. This is the easy usage of the 'select' loop. The 'select' loop construct is like 'for' loop. What it does is reads the list first and displays the menu's structure, and then we can select any item from the menu. Based on the selected menu, the command executes given in 'do' and 'done' keywords. Also, you can see it does not end the script; it is still prompting the number. To end the script, press ctrl=c.

The 'select' loop is often used with the 'case' statement. We can use some cases with the 'select' loop; we will see how to use it.

Between keyword do and done, we will start the basic structure of 'case'. With the case, we write the variable 'name' and keyword 'in'.

```
do
    case $name in
```

Now we will create the case statement based on the four names we have given in the list. First, let's create a case for the name 'mark' and assign an 'echo' command to display the message that 'mark selected'. Similarly, we will create a case for all four names as below:

```
    mark)
       echo mark selected ;;
    john)
       echo john selected ;;
    tom)
       echo tom selected ;;
    ben)
       echo ben selected ;;
```

In the last, we will create the default 'case' with the asterisk symbol (*) to display an error message and print some text. This will execute if it does not select the number between 1 to 4. With this, close the 'case' statement by keyword 'esac'.

```
   *)
       echo "Error, please provide the number between 1..4"
   esac
done
```

The script will become like below:

```
#! /bin/bash

select name in mark john tom ben
do
   case $name in
   mark)
       echo mark selected ;;
   john)
       echo john selected ;;
   tom)
       echo tom selected ;;
   ben)
       echo ben selected ;;
   *)
       echo "Error, please provide the number between 1..4"
   esac
done
```

Let's execute the script.

```
$ ./hello.sh
1) mark
2) john
3) tom
4) ben
```

```
#? 4
ben selected
#? 2
john selected
#? 3
tom selected
#? 1
mark selected
#? 7
Error, please provide the number between 1..4
#?
```

Here you can see that the script will keep prompting the number, and the command is getting executed that is associated with the number we are proving as input. This way 'select' loop is often used with 'case'. In the example we are using a simple 'echo' command, but you can provide any complex logic based upon the selected value from the select loop.

This is the primary usage of 'select' loop usage.

Summary:

We learned how to use the 'select' loop, its syntax. The simple format of using it. Also learned how to use it with 'case'.

CHAPTER 16

Break and Continue

In this chapter, we will learn how to use 'break' statement and 'continue' statement.

Break Statement

A break statement is used to exit the current loop before its normal execution. Whenever we want to break out the loop prematurely, then we can use a break statement. Let's understand this with an example.

Below is the script of 'for' loop:

```
#! /bin/bash

for (( v=1 ; v<=10 ; v++ ))
do
        echo "$v"
done
```

In this script, it initializes the value of variable 'v' as 1, and then we are waiting for the condition of value 'v' is less than or equal to 10, and last, we are incrementing the value by 1. This we have learned in detail in previous chapters. Between 'do' and 'done', we run the 'echo' command to print the value of 'v'. Let's run the script and see how it works.

```
$ ./hello.sh
1
2
3
4
5
6
7
8
9
10
$
```

This a normal operation that we have learned. Now for some reasons, we want to come out of the loop prematurely; when the value of 'v' is greater than 5, then we want to come out of the loop.

To do this, we will start 'if' condition under 'do' by defining that if its value is greater than 5, then we want to come out of the loop. Under 'then', we will use the command 'break' to end the loop.

```
if [ $v -gt 5 ]
then
        break
fi
```

What it does is, whenever the value of 'v' goes greater than 5, then the condition is true in 'if' statement. Next, it comes to 'then' and it execute the program 'break', and it comes out of the loop. Now the complete script will be as below:

```
#! /bin/bash

for (( v=1 ; v<=10 ; v++ ))
do
        if [ $v -gt 5 ]
        then
                break
        fi
```

```
        echo "$v"
done
```

Let's execute the script.

```
$ ./hello.sh
1
2
3
4
5
$
```

Now, as expected, it has printed the values from 1 to 5. When the condition is true that 'v' is greater than 5, keyword 'break' is called, and the program comes out of the loop.

We have seen, though 'for' loop has a condition to print the numbers up to 10, but we have given a special keyword 'break'. It makes when the 'if' statement is true, it ends the loop.

This way, you can break the normal execution of the loop prematurely. Now next, let's see how to use the 'continue' statement.

Continue Statement

The 'continue' is different from 'break'. When we use 'continue', it skips the normal execution for that statement, so whatever comes after the 'continue' word will be skipped, and the program will go to the next statement.

To explain this, we will change the previous script. Let's change the value of 'v' from 5 to 3. The condition greater than –gt will be changed to equal to –eq, and we will also add OR operation. The second condition after OR is where it checks the value of 'v' is equal to 6 –eq. The 'if' condition will look as below:

```
if [ $v -eq 3 OR $v -eq 6 ]
```

If the condition is true, then the 'continue' statement will execute whenever there is the input of value 3 or 6. The complete script will look as below:

```
#! /bin/bash

for (( v=1 ; v<=10 ; v++ ))
do
        if [ $v -eq 3 OR $v -eq 6 ]
        then
                continue
        fi
        echo "$v"
done
```

Let's execute the script now.

```
$ ./hello.sh
1
2
4
5
7
8
9
10
$
```

Here we can see it print the numbers from 1 to 10. If you look closely, numbers 3 and 6 are missing. That means whenever the condition is met where v=3 or v=6, then the keyword 'continue' is called. So whenever your program sees this keyword in a loop, then whatever comes after this keyword will be skipped.

In this script, 'echo comes after 'continue' keyword. That means if it meet then the condition which makes 'echo' command to skip and the program will go to the next attrition. So when number 3 or 6 comes, that time condition is met which makes the 'continue' statement is called, and the 'echo' command is skipped. This makes it will not print these two numbers.

Summary:

In this chapter, we learned about break statements, and continue statements, their syntax to use with examples.

CHAPTER 17

Functions

A function is a subroutine or a code block that implements a set of operations. For a user, it is like a black box; it has some name on it, and it implements some functionality. Later, users can use this function once or multiple times. Like any other language, Linux scripting also supports function, though it has some limited implementations.

There are two ways with which we can use function.

Method 1

```
Function name(){
     Commands
}
```

For this notation, we use the keyword 'function', and then we assign a name to the function followed by parenthesis with the start of the curly bracket. Next, we execute some commands.

Method 2

```
name () {
     Commands
}
```

In this method, first, we assign the name of the function followed by a parenthesis and a curly bracket. Next, there will be commands.

We will see both notations and how to use it.

We want to print 'hello world' using the 'function'. For method 1, first, we will give a name to the function; in our case we are giving a name as 'Hello'. We will write commands between curly brackets. For this example, we will run command 'echo' to display 'Hello'.

```
function Hello(){
        echo "Hello"
}
```

Let's create another function; whenever we call it, it will quit the script. Now let's name this function as 'quit'. This function will just be called command 'exit' which will exit the shell script.

```
quit () {
        exit
}
```

Now we have two functions in the script as below:

```
#! /bin/bash

function Hello(){
        echo "Hello"
}
quit () {
        exit
}
```

Let's execute the script having two functions:

```
$ ./hello.sh
$
```

Nothing came up. Though we have created the functions but haven't used them.

Let's use these functions in the script now.

First, we will use 'hello' function to print something. To use a function in the script, you can call it. To call the function, write the name of the function. First, we will call the function 'Hello' by writing 'Hello'. Script will be as below:

```
#! /bin/bash

function Hello(){
        echo "Hello"
}
quit () {
        exit
}
Hello
```

Let's execute the script

```
$ ./hello.sh
Hello
$
```

Now the script has printed 'Hello' as we have called only 'Hello' function. Now let's call our second function, that is 'quit' function.

We will call the function 'quit' before 'Hello' and after Hello. Also, we are adding another command 'echo' to print some text. The script will be as below:

```
#! /bin/bash

function Hello(){
        echo "Hello"
}
quit () {
        exit
}
quit
```

```
Hello
echo "dummy text."
```

Let's execute the script now.

```
$ ./hello.sh
$
```

Nothing came up. This has happened because we called 'quit' function first, which has executed the exit command and ended the script. The function Hello and the echo command could not execute.

Let's change the sequence now. We will first call 'Hello' function then 'quit' and at last echo command as below:

```
#! /bin/bash

function Hello(){
        echo "Hello"
}
quit () {
        exit
}
Hello
quit
echo "dummy text."
```

We will execute the script now

```
$ ./hello.sh
Hello
$
```

This time Hello is printed but echo command is not. This has happened because of the sequence we have given. Hello function worked fine, but before echo command, we have provided the 'quit' function, which has called 'exit' command, and it has terminated the script.

Now let's use the quit function after the echo command. The sequence will be first Hello function, then echo command and finally quit function. The script will become as below:

```
#! /bin/bash

function Hello(){
        echo "Hello"
}
quit () {
        exit
}
Hello
echo "dummy text."
quit
```

Let's execute the script now

```
$ ./hello.sh
Hello
dummy text
$
```

This time first hello function has executed and made Hello message to display, then the echo command to print the text, finally the quit function to run exit command.

This has been explained well that it can make the function declaration in any sequence, but calling of the function sequence matters for the behavior of the script.

Next, let's learn how we can pass an argument to a function.

Let's change the name of the function Hello to print. To prompt argument by the function, echo command can do this with a $1 function. The $1 means one argument if we have $2, $3, etc. that means the second and third argument.

```
function print(){
        echo $1
```

Now next is to understand how we can give an argument to the function print. That can be done by simply writing an argument after we call the function on the same line as below. For example, with function print, we want to call an argument 'Hello' as shown below

```
print Hello
```

So when the function print is called in script, the word 'Hello' will go as an argument in echo command as the value of $1. This will print the word 'Hello'. Now the script will be as below:

```
#! /bin/bash

function print(){
        echo $1
}
quit () {
        exit
}
print Hello
echo "dummy text."
quit
```

Now let's execute the script

```
$ ./hello.sh
Hello
dummy text
$
```

Now Hello is printing from the print function and 'dummy text' printed from 'echo' command. We can also call function multiple times, and they may be different arguments. Let's call print function two times with different arguments:

```
#! /bin/bash

function print(){
        echo $1
}
quit () {
        exit
}
print Hello
print World
print Again
echo "dummy text."
quit
```

Let's execute the script now.

```
$ ./hello.sh
Hello
World
Again
dummy text
$
```

This has come as expected. This way we can call the function multiple times with multiple arguments

Now let's add two more arguments for print functions as $2 and $3. When the print function is called, we will write three arguments there. Now it should print all the three arguments. The script will be as below:

```
#! /bin/bash

function print(){
        echo $1 $2 $3
}
quit () {
        exit
}
```

```
print Hello World Again
echo "dummy text."
quit
```

Let's execute the script now.

```
$ ./hello.sh
Hello World Again
dummy text
$
```

It prints all three words on the same line as it captures these by three variables $1, $2, and $3.

Summary:

We understood the functionality of the 'function', the syntax, and its use. We also learned that the sequence of function created does not matter; the sequence in which we call function in script matters. Got the introduction to the ways to add arguments to the function.

CHAPTER 18

Local Variables

Until now, we understood the simple functions, now let's learn functions in a bit more detail. By default, every variable which you define in a script is a global variable, which means that it can be accessed from anywhere from your script. First, let's understand why we need a local variable and how to use it.

See the below script we have saw in the previous chapter:

```
#! /bin/bash

function print(){
        echo $1
}
print Hello

echo "dummy text."

quit
```

Here we have a function 'print,' which will have one argument for variable $1. The function 'print' is called with an argument 'Hello', and then an echo command prints the text. When this script executes, the word 'Hello' will be assigned to a variable $1.

Let's say we want to use this function to print a name, so we will declare a variable name in this function, and the value of this variable will be out the first argument, which is $1. Let's modify the echo command with more text as below. In the argument, we are giving the name 'Max' here. The script will be as below now.

```
#! /bin/bash

function print(){
        name=$1
        echo "the name is $name"
}
print Max

echo "dummy text."
```

Let's execute the script now.

```
$ ./hello.sh
the name is Max
dummy text
```

It prints 'the name is Max,' which is correct. The name 'Max' was assigned to variable $1. It assigns the first argument to variable 'name' and echo will print the value of the 'name,

We just read above that all variables are global in a shell script, so the variable name can be declared at any other line as well. In the script, before calling the function 'print' let's write variable 'name' again with value 'Tom', and in the next line, we can run echo command to type text to print the name. Now the script will be as below:

#! /bin/bash

```
function print(){
        name=$1
```

```
        echo "the name is $name"
}
name="Tom"
echo "The name is $name."
print Max
echo "dummy text."
```

Let's execute the script and see what happens.

```
$ ./hello.sh
The name is Tom
the name is Max
dummy text
```

Now first, it says 'The name is Tom' because first, we have assigned the variable name value as Tom. The function was created before, but until the time function is not called, it will not be executed, it will just sit ideal. So the shell script starts execution from the line where we set the variable 'name' and assigned the value as Tom. After that the 'print' function will be called with argument as Max. Now the 'print' function will set this as the value of variable $1, and next to the echo command will print the value as Max. Next, the echo command will print the value of this variable set.

What it tells us is that the variable name 'name' where we defined it as the 'Tom' is a global variable name, as we can access it from anywhere in the script. Sometimes we want the variable we define in the function should remain as a local variable; it should not change outside the function. That is where the 'local' command comes in. Whenever you add 'local' command, the variable becomes local. We can use it only inside the function. To define a local variable in function, add 'local' keyword before the variable name as shown below:

```
function print(){
        local name=$1
        echo "the name is $name"
```

We will show you how the 'local' keyword works in script in detail later in this chapter. For that first, let's see how the script works before adding the 'local' keyword.

Now we are working on the same script as shown before. Another echo command is being added after 'print Max'. Now the echo command is there before and after the print function. We will mark 'Before' and 'After' as a comment in both the echo commands, as shown below.

```
#! /bin/bash

function print(){
        name=$1
        echo "the name is $name"
}
name="Tom"
echo "The name is $ name: Before."
print Max
echo "The name is $ name: After."
```

Let's execute the script and understand what the output means.

```
$ ./hello.sh
The name is Tom: Before
the name is Max
The name is Max: After
```

Now let's understand every line.

- The first line of output: "The name is Tom: Before":

    This output has come as the first variable set with the below two lines in the script:

    ```
    name="Tom"
    echo "The name is $ name: Before."
    ```

This has been printed before the 'print' function was called, which is correct.

- The second line of output: "the name is Max."

This line has been printed as the 'print' function was called with an argument 'Max'. When the 'print' function was called, then in that function, the variable 'name' has been set its value as 'Max'.

- The third line of output : "The name is Max : After."

In the previous step, the variable 'name' has been assigned with the value 'Max'. With the echo command when it prints text for the variable 'name', it reads as 'Max' only. Now until any change is done in the variable value, it keeps the value as 'Max' throughout.

This is a bit confusing, as we have set the variable name as 'Tom' initially, which is outside our function. We expect the variable defined in function should not change the value defined outside the function which a global name. That means in the second echo command we expect output as Tom' only. This requirement of keeping the same variable value which is a global and should not be changed by any variable defined in the function. This where 'local' keyword comes in the picture.

Let's do a change in the 'print' function we will define keyword 'local' before the variable is defined. Now the script will look as below:

```
#! /bin/bash

function print(){
        local name=$1
        echo "the name is $name"
}
name="Tom"
```

```
echo "The name is $name : Before."
print Max
echo "The name is $name : After."
```

Let's execute the script now.

```
$ ./hello.sh
The name is Tom : Before
the name is Max
The name is Tom : After
```

You can see when the keyword 'local' has been added in front of the variable; then this variable has become a local, it cannot access the variable outside the function. This will be just for local execution and will not affect the global variable.

How every line of output has come, let's understand now.

- The first line of output: `The name is Tom : Before`

  This is output from the 1st echo command. Before this echo command, the value of the global variable 'name' was set as 'Tom'.

- The second line of output: `the name is Max`

  At this stage, the function 'print' was called with argument Max. In this function, the variable value of 'name' has been set as the argument provided and it printed it as 'Max. The variable this time is from the function 'print' was set with 'kcyword' local.

- The third line of output: `The name is Tom : After`

  This time again, echo command has been executed to print the variable 'name'. Now the script is picking the value of variable, which is set as a global variable that is 'Tom'. The echo command will not pick the local variable which was set in the 'print' function.

In short, the local variables will be defined in a function and will be used only in the places where the function is called. All the places when the variable is called, i uses the value that is set as a global variable. This is how the local and global variables can be differentiated and can be used in practice in the script.

Now let's understand an example to consolidate the learnings of function. With this example, you will get clear on more concept

In the example, we will create small sections and explain each section; in the end, we will combine all the sections to make a complete meaningful script. So you might need to reread this section to have more clarity.

To Check if the File Exists or Not using our Script. Whenever the user runs the script, it has to be the file name as an argument for which the script is being run. The script will check if the file exists or not, and it will print. We have seen this in previous chapters also which can do this task, but now we will use the function and learn more concepts.

Section 1: Create a function name 'is_file_exist'

```
is_file_exist() {
        local file="$1"
```

We will create a function with name 'is_file_exist' in the format it has to be used. We have to pass the name of the file when we call this function as an argument; it will be defined as a local variable. The variable name will be 'file', and its value will be an argument $1. This we have learned in the previous section.

Section 2:

```
            --- 1st cond. of AND ---   AND ------2nd cond. of AND -------
            [[ -f "file" ]] && return 0 || return 1
                        --- 1st cond.--- OR   ---2nd cond---
```

In this section, we will use AND operator, OR operator, and –f flag to verify if the file exists or not.

This will be a part of the function that we are writing. We want to check if the file exists for that we will use AND operator format. A double square bracket having –f flag checks whether the mentioned filename is a file or directory. Next to –f, we will write the file variable that we defined as a local variable $file. This will become a 1st condition of AND operator. It will show if the file exists or not. Until now, we have completed the 1st part of AND condition. Now let see the 2nd condition.

Note we have not given 'if' condition, now we will use return value. If you know any programming language, you might be familiar with ternary operations. We are checking whether the operation is true; depending on the result, if it is true, it will return some value, and if it is false, then it will return some other value. We will use double AND operator (&&) and keyword return0 and return 1. Between 'return 0' and 'return 1' there will be OR operator (||)

So what is happening here is, if the file exists, then the 1st condition is true; that means the output is 1. When the output is 1, it will go to check the next condition – 'return 0 || return 1'. Since the file exists, that means the result is 1, so it will go to return 1. If the argument is not given or that file is not there, that means the result is 0. In that case, when it will check the 2nd condition on AND, it will go to 'return 0'.

Section 3: Create a function with name 'usage'.

```
usage () {
        echo "You need to provide an argument : "
        echo "usage : $0 file_name"
```

We will provide the name of the function 'usage'; then, two echo commands to print two messages. First message is to print the message "you need to provide an argument". In a second echo message, we will give the name of the script that will be done by $0 and the filename by file_name.

Section 4: In this section, we will check if the user has given any argument or not with the shell scripting.

```
[[ $# -eq 0 ]] && usage
--------cond 1-----------      AND    --cond 2--
```

This line also has an AND operator; the first condition is validating if the number of arguments provided is not zero. The second condition will call the usage function that we created in section 3 above.

If you remember, the $# will get the count number of arguments that are given with the script. Next, if the number is equal to (-eq) zero, in that case, we want to show a message to the user. For that, we will go the next section of AND operator, which is calling function 'usage'.

Section 5: Creating an 'if' statement

```
if (is_file_exist "$1")
then
        echo "File found"
else
        echo "File not found"
fi
```

Now here in if we are writing an expression by setting variable name as 'is_file_exist' with value as $1. IMPORTANT to note here that in 'if' statement we have given name as 'is_file_exist', this means we are calling the function that we have created in section 1. Next is the $1, this is the argument that we have provided to the script.

In short:

$1 used in 'if' variable is the argument that we will give with the script

$1 used in the function of a local variable of is_file_exist function as the first argument

So both $1 mentioned in the script are different.

Now combining all the sections and below will be the script.

```
#! /bin/bash

usage () {
        echo "You need to provide an argument : "
        echo "usage : $0 file_name"
}
is_file_exist() {
        local file="$1"
        [[ -f "$file" ]] && return 0 || return 1
}
[[ $# -eq 0 ]] && usage
if (is_file_exist "$1")
then
        echo "File found"
else
        echo "File not found"
fi
```

Before we execute the script, let's list the files in the current directory:

```
$ ls -l
total 32
drwxr-xr-x 2 user1 users       6 Nov 15 17:20 backup
-rw-r--r-- 1 user1 users     454 Nov 15 16:37 doc
-rw-r--r-- 1 user1 users     501 Nov 15 16:38 examples
-rw-r--r-- 1 user1 users       0 Nov 15 16:38 glass
-rwxr-xr-x 1 user1 users     291 Nov 16 23:54 hello.sh
```

```
-rwxr-xr-x 1 user1 users    357 Nov 11 22:15
hello.sh.org
drwxr-xr-x 2 user1 users      6 Nov 15 16:34 myhome
-rw-r--r-- 1 user1 users  13336 Nov 15 16:39 scripts
drwxr-xr-x 2 user1 users      6 Nov 15 16:34 test
```

Now first, let's execute the script. It is expected to provide an argument with the script, but first, we will execute the script with no argument.

```
$ ./hello.sh
You need to provide an argument :
usage : ./hello.sh file_name
File not found
```

This has given a message to provide an argument and also the usage instructions to provide the file_name after the script name.

Let's execute the script again with a filename as an argument.

```
$ ./hello.sh glass
File found
```

Now it gives a successful message

So what we have learned mainly are two things from this example:

1. First, the $1 in function is_file_exist, and $1 in 'if' statement is different. The $1 with 'if' statement is the variable that is provided as an argument with the script to execute. And $1 in function is the one which is provided to the function as a local variable.

2. Second, we learned how to use AND and OR operator without 'if' condition in section 2. We could have used 'if' conditions, but it could have taken many more lines. If you are not comfortable with the way explained in section 2, you can use it with normal 'if' conditions.

CHAPTER 19

Read Only Command

In this chapter, we will learn how to use a read-only command in shell scripting. Read Only variables can be used with variables and functions. With the name only we can understand that it can use to make variables and functions read-only and cannot be overwritten.

The syntax to write read-only command is

```
readonly <variable name>
```

Let's understand with an example. We will write a variable 'var' with value as 31. Now we can use 'read-only' command on this variable. For that, write read-only, followed by a variable name. Once this is set, in the next line, we will write the same variable with a different value. It is shown below:

```
#! /bin/bash

var=31
readonly var
var=50
```

Let's execute the script now:

```
$ ./hello.sh
./hello.sh: line 7: var: readonly variable
$
```

It gives us a warning that 'var' is a read-only variable. Let's print the value of var in the script

```
#! /bin/bash

var=31
readonly var
var=50
echo "var => $var"
```

Execute the script now.

```
$ ./hello.sh
./hello.sh: line 7: var: readonly variable
var => 31
$
```

The value of var is still 31, though we have reassign the value of var to 50, but it remains the same with the first value assigned. This has happened as we have made var variable as read-only, and any other value cannot be assigned. When we try to assign another value, it displays a warning.

The same way we can make functions also read-only. First, let's create a function name, hello to print message hello. We will add the function in our previous script.

```
#! /bin/bash

var=31
readonly var
var=50
echo "var => $var"
hello() {
        echo "Hello World"
}
Hello
```

Let's execute the script now.

```
$ ./hello.sh
./hello.sh: line 7: var: readonly variable
var => 31
Hello World
$
```

You can see the message 'Hello World' is printed. Now, if we want to make this function read-only. For that, we will use the read-only keyword with function, but this will not make function as required. For function, we need to use the flag –f.

```
readonly -f <function name>
```

Let's make the function 'hello' as read-only in our script. Let's make this function as read-only in our script, and then we will try to change the value by adding lines for the same function with different echo command. Below is the script now:

```
#! /bin/bash

var=31
readonly var
var=50
echo "var => $var"
hello() {
        echo "Hello World"
}
readonly -f hello
hello() {
        echo "Hello World Again"
}
```

Let's execute the script now:

```
$ ./hello.sh
./hello.sh: line 7: var: readonly variable
var => 31
```

```
./hello.sh: line 19: hello: readonly function
```

We can see the message has come for the function hello that it is read-only.

Let's do one more test. What will happen if we write the keyword 'readonly' without defining any variable or function? Let's add this keyword to our script and do this test.

```
#! /bin/bash

readonly
```

Let's execute the script now:

```
$ ./hello.sh
```

BASHOPTS="checkwinsize:cmdhist:complete_fullquote:extquote:force_fignore:hostcomplete:interactive_comments:progcomp:promptvars:sourcepath"

```
declare -ir BASHPID
declare -ar BASH_VERSINFO=([0]="4" [1]="4" [2]="23" [3]="1" [4]="release" [5]="x86_64-suse-linux-gnu")
declare -ir EUID="1001"
declare -ir PPID="11356"
declare -r:
SHELLOPTS="braceexpand:hashall:interactive-comments"
declare -ir UID="1001"
$
```

Now, what can we see is the list; all variables which are built-in and read-only. These are:

BASHOPTS, BASHPID, BASH_VERSINFO, EUID, PPID, SHELLOPTS and UID.

If you want to see all read-only functions, then in script, we will write read-only with the flag –f. First, let's create a function in the script and make it read-only.

```
#! /bin/bash

hello() {
        echo "Hello"
}
readonly -f hello
readonly -f
```

Let's execute now:

```
$ ./hello.sh
hello ()
{
    echo "Hello"
}
declare -fr hello
$
```

In the output, the read-only function is printed.

Summary:

We learned how we could make variable and function as read-only. Once it is made as read-only, we cannot reassign to another value.

We learned how to display read-only variables and functions.

CHAPTER 20

Signals and Traps

When any script is running to compete, all steps written in it, and during its processing, it gets an instruction to stop the execution. This interruption is called a signal. In signal terms, it is called SIGINT. It will be more transparent with an example.

We have created a script below.

```
#! /bin/bash

echo "pid is $$"
while (( COUNT < 10 ))
do
        sleep 10
        (( COUNT ++ ))
        echo $COUNT
done
exit 0
```

In this script, 1st with echo command, it is checking PID (process ID) of the script itself that is assigned in the system. The variable $$ will get the PID of the script. After that, the 'while' loop starts with a condition for the COUNT to be less than 10. In 'do', there is a sleep of 10 seconds; after every one cycle of the loop, for the next execution, the loop will suspend for 10 seconds and increment the number by 1. In this way, the script will run until the count reaches ten after that script will be ended. The total runtime of the script will be 100 seconds.

```
$ ./hello.sh
pid is 16245
1
2
3
4
5
6
^C
$
```

Here the script has started with PID as 16245, and every count is printed on the screen at the interval of 10 seconds. Now while running the script, some scenarios can happen. Users can press ctrl+c to come out of the script. Here in the above example, we have pressed crtl+c to terminate the script while it was in the middle of processing. In this case, we have provided crtl+c SIGNAL, and this is called an interrupted signal, and in a signal term, it is called SIGINT. So we have sent SIGINT command to terminate the script in between before its completion.

Let's rerun the same script and do one more test to understand more options.

```
$ ./hello.sh
pid is 16269
1
2
3
4
5
^Z
[1]+  Stopped                 ./hello.sh
$
```

The PID of the script now is 16269. This time in place of pressing ctrl+c, we have pressed ctrl+z to terminate the script. The ctrl+z is called a suspend signal; in signal term, it is called SIGTSTP. When we pressed ctrl+z, the script gave the message 'Stopped' and this is also an interrupt signal as the script was in the middle of doing something

Let's understand interrupting the process with the kill command. Let's execute the script again.

The PID of the script now is 16481. While script is running, open a new terminal, and run command kill to end this process using PID. Run the below command in another terminal

```
$ kill -9 16481
```

The option -9 is also is a signal, and it is called SIGKILL, and 16481 is the PID. As soon as we give the kill command. We will see on the terminal where the script was running, that it got ended with a message 'killed', and the script is stopped. It is shown below:

```
$ ./hello.sh
pid is 16481
1
2
3
4
Killed
$
```

In this way there will be scenarios when the script is interrupted, means while script was running some interruption signal can come or some unexpected behavior can stop the execution. This is where we use command - trap.

The complete list of signals is listed in the man page of signal. Run command man seven signal, and if you scroll, there will be a complete list of the signals. That is shown below:

Signal	Value	Action	Comment
SIGHUP	1	Term	Hangup detected on controlling terminal or death of controlling process
SIGINT	2	Term	Interrupt from keyboard
SIGQUIT	3	Core	Quit from keyboard
SIGILL	4	Core	Illegal Instruction
SIGABRT	6	Core	Abort signal from abort(3)
SIGFPE	8	Core	Floating-point exception
SIGKILL	9	Term	Kill signal
SIGSEGV	11	Core	Invalid memory reference
SIGPIPE	13	Term	Broken pipe: write to pipe with no readers; see pipe(7)
SIGALRM	14	Term	Timer signal from alarm(2)
SIGTERM	15	Term	Termination signal
SIGUSR1	30,10,16	Term	User-defined signal
SIGUSR2	31,12,17	Term	User-defined signal 2
SIGCHLD	20,17,18	Ign	Child stopped or terminated
SIGCONT	19,18,25	Cont	Continue if stopped
SIGSTOP	17,19,23	Stop	Stop process
SIGTSTP	18,20,24	Stop	Stop typed at terminal
SIGTTIN	21,21,26	Stop	Terminal input for background process
SIGTTOU	22,22,27	Stop	Terminal output for background process

In the above table, we can see, when the ctrl+c was processed, that was an interruption from the keyboard and had a signal name as SIGINT As listed in the table. It has value of 2.

Next, we have pressed ctrl+z. When we did that, we could see 'stop' was typed on the screen. As per table, that will be SIGTSTP with value 12, 20 and 24.

In the third example, we terminated the script using 'kill' command, which means there was a signal SIGKILL. It has value 9. When we gave the kill command, we have mentioned this value as -9

To get more details about the signal, you can run below command

```
$ man seven signal
```

Trap Command

Why we use trap command? When a script is running, and it is interrupted in between without the completion of the project, that time trap command is used to capture the interrupt and then clean it up within the script.

Let's understand with an example. We will have the script below:

```
#! /bin/bash

trap "echo Exit command is detected" 0
echo "Hello world"
exit 0
```

The script starts with a trap command, and then we will echo some text that "Exit command is detected". After that, we will type 0; this is a signal what we expect. Signal 0 means success. We have seen the value of signals in the table, and the values are always greater than 0. At the end, 0 means it is a success.

The next line has an echo to print text 'Hello World', and the last line is that we want to exit from the script, so we gave exit 0. The 'exit 0' is a success signal.

Let's execute the script now.

```
$ ./hello.sh
Hello world
Exit command is detected
$
```

Let's understand the sequence of execution of the script. It has started with a command trap for a signal. The trap means whenever it receives the signal 0, then it will execute the command, which is written in quotes. In our case after trap written is "echo Exit command is detected". Here command echo is used to print the text. In the end, 0 means to print this when this signal is found in the script. This is on the third line as 'exit 0'.

To understand more, let's see our old script again as below:

```
#! /bin/bash

echo "pid is $$."
while (( COUNT < 10 ))
do
        sleep 10
        (( COUNT ++ ))
        echo $COUNT
done
exit 0
```

We will make some changes here now. We will add trap command with the text in echo. At the end of the trap line, we want to detect a SIGINT signal; then, this word will be written in the end. To mention SIGINT, it can be written either by the name of a signal or by its value 2. SIGINT is an interruption by a keyboard that is ctrl+c. By adding this line, the script will be as below:

```
#! /bin/bash

trap "echo Exit command is detected" SIGINT
echo "pid is $$"
while (( COUNT < 10 ))
do
        sleep 10
        (( COUNT ++ ))
        echo $COUNT
done
exit 0
```

Let's execute the script now, and while it is executing, we will press ctrl+c and see what happens.

```
$ ./hello.sh
pid is 18741
1
2
3
4
^CExit command is detected
5
6
^CExit command is detected
7
^CExit command is detected
8
^CExit command is detected
9
^CExit command is detected
10
$
```

We can see that script started with PID 18741, and after counter 4, we pressed ctrl+c and messages printed on-screen "^CExit command is detected". This is the message we wrote in the trap with echo command. The interesting thing is even we have pressed ctrl+c, the script is not ending up. We pressed crtl+c multiple times, and every time the same message was printed, but the script didn't terminate. It has completed its counter and then ended.

Let's try to trap the SIGKILL signal. So do this, with trap command we will mention SIGKILL or its value as 9

```
#! /bin/bash

trap "echo Exit command is detected" SIGKILL
echo "pid is $$"
while (( COUNT < 10 ))
do
        sleep 2
        (( COUNT ++ ))
        echo $COUNT
done
exit 0
```

Let's execute the script. When the script is running, we will open another terminal and run kill -9 <PID>. It will generate PID when we start the script.

```
$ ./hello.sh
pid is 18816
1
2
3
Killed
$
```

When the script was executing, we opened another session and ran the command kill -9 18816 (18816 is the PID). This time the executing of script got ended with the message 'killed', we did not saw the text message written in trap command. Why has this happened? The command trap was supposed to print the message written in echo.

There are some exceptions to the trap. The trap command cannot capture the SIGKILL and SIGSTOP command. So anytime when SIGKILL or SIGSTOP is used, the trap cannot catch these signals. It is recommended not to use SIGKILL or SIGSTOP for trap command.

Now we will see more examples and see how it works.

This time we want that when a signal is received, it will delete a file. Let's do it now.

First, let's check the files in our directory and creating a new empty file with touch command

```
$ ls
hello.sh
$ pwd
/home/user1/
$ touch test
$ ls
hello.sh   test
$
```

We want we will define a signal in our script, and when that signal is received, it should delete the file we create 'test'. To do this, we will create a variable in our script 'file' and to give its value, we will define its complete path of the file name 'test' as shown below:

```
file="/home/user1/test"
```

Another change we will do in trap command. In place of echo, command, we will add command rm –f with the file variable name that is $file. Also, on the same line, we write that after deleting this file exit the script. This can be done by writing exit. Also, we want to catch the success signal as 0 (SUCCESS), 2 (SIGINT), and 15 (SIGTERM). The line will become as below:

```
trap "rm -f $file ; exit" 0 2 15
```

The semicolon symbol (;) is used to combine two commands. Now the trap will delete the file when it receives any of these three signals.

Now the script will be as below:

```
#! /bin/bash

file=/home/user1/test
trap "rm -f $file; exit" 0 2 15
echo "pid is $$"
while (( COUNT < 10 ))
do
        sleep 5
        (( COUNT ++ ))
        echo $COUNT
done
exit 0
```

We will execute the script now, and when the script is going through execution, we will send the signals which will delete the file. Since we can see the PID, we will use another terminal to run kill command with the number of the signal

Terminal 1: After counter three kill command issues from terminal 2

```
$ ./hello.sh
pid is 19483
1
2
3
$
```

Terminal 2: Kill command issued and check the list of the file

```
$ kill -15 19483
$ ls
hello.sh
```

Here we can see, when the kill command issued with value 15, the script got terminated. Also, we checked the listing of files by ls command we found that file 'test' got deleted.

Let's play with script more. With rm command, we will add a AND operator - && and run echo command with text "file deleted", so we know that trap is executed.

Once again, we will create the file 'test' with touch command the file test.

Now the script will be as below:

```
#! /bin/bash

file=/home/user1/test
trap "rm -f $file && echo file deleted; exit" 0 2 15
echo "pid is $$"
while (( COUNT < 10 ))
do
        sleep 5
        (( COUNT ++ ))
        echo $COUNT
done
exit 0
```

Again like earlier, we will execute the script in terminal 1, and on terminal 2, we will issue the kill -15 PID command. As soon as the command is issued, on terminal 1 'file deleted' message should be printed.

Terminal 1: Executed the script and got the message as soon as the kill command was issued from terminal 2

```
$ ./hello.sh
pid is 22758
1
2
3
```

```
4
file deleted
file deleted
$
```

Terminal 2: First created the file 'test' before the script was executed in terminal 1. After the script started, the command kill -15 was issued and checked the file; it is deleted.

```
$ ls
hello.sh
$ touch test
$ ls
hello.sh   test
$ kill -15 22758
$ ls
hello.sh
$
```

We can see the message 'file deleted' messaged was printed on terminal 1, where the script was getting executed.

So you can use any command in the trap when the signal is received.

Let's see one scenario of the trap. The file is deleted; now, we will execute the script again on one terminal and on another terminal, we will run a command trap without any argument or a flag.

Terminal 1: Executing the script

```
$ ./hello.sh
pid is 22970
1
2
3
4
5
```

Terminal 2: Running the trap command

```
$ trap
trap -- '' SIGTSTP
trap -- '' SIGTTIN
trap -- '' SIGTTOU
```

We saw that in output, there is a list of traps. These traps are from our script. If any other trap script is also executing in the system that will also be listed here. In some cases, even the script is over still, it will list here. Let's understand how to remove traps. To remove the traps below is the syntax.

```
$ trap - trap value or name
```

Let's remove the trap from the system by running the below command

```
$ trap - 0 2 15
```

This command will remove the three traps which we in the list. Once this is executed and you recheck the trap command, it will be blank.

Summary:

We learned the usage of Signal and Trap command with examples. We understood the two exceptions of tarp command – SIGKILL and SIGSTOP.

We learned how to delete the files with trap command.

How to clear the traps from the system.

CHAPTER 21

How to Debug Script

In this chapter, we will learn to debug the script. Sometimes when the things are not going as planned, we need to determine what is causing the script to fail. There are features built in the shell to debug. The most common is start a subshell with –x option.

To understand this, we will use the script in the last chapter:

```
1  #! /bin/bash
2
3  file=/home/user1/test
4  trap "rm -f $file && echo file deleted; exit" 0 2 15
5
6  echo "pid is $$"
7  while (( COUNT < 10 )
8  do
9          sleep 10
10         (( COUNT ++ ))
11         echo $COUNT
12 done
13 exit 0
```

We have checked in the previous chapter that this script will work well. Let's say we missed to put double parenthesis in while loop

```
 1  #! /bin/bash
 2
 3  file=/home/user1/test
 4  trap "rm -f $file && echo file deleted; exit" 0 2 15
 5
 6  echo "pid is $$"
 7  while (( COUNT < 10 )
 8  do
 9          sleep 10
10          (( COUNT ++ ))
11          echo $COUNT
12  done
13  exit 0
```

Now when we execute the script we get error as below:

```
$ ./hello.sh
pid is 23323
./hello.sh: line 12: syntax error near unexpected token `done'
./hello.sh: line 12: `done'
file deleted
$
```

This is a straight forward message "syntax error near unexpected token `done'" on line 12. Though the problem is in while loop, it has shown the error for line 12 for 'done', but still, it is very close. But if you want to debug it more, then you can use the "-x" option. Every script has its tools for debugging. For bash below syntax can be used:

```
$ bash -x <script name>
```

Let's execute this command for our script.

```
$ ./hello.sh
pid is 23323
```

```
./hello.sh: line 12: syntax error near unexpected
token `done'
./hello.sh: line 12: `done'
file deleted
$ bash -x ./hello.sh
+ file=/home/user1/test
+ trap 'rm -f /home/user1/test && echo file deleted;
exit' 0 2 15
+ echo 'pid is 23349'
pid is 23349
./hello.sh: line 12: syntax error near unexpected
token `done'
./hello.sh: line 12: `done'
+ rm -f /home/user1/test
+ echo file deleted
file deleted
+ exit
$
```

Now we can see it more verbose and getting more detail for each line. It is showing the execution of each line in detail and will help to debug around which line the error is coming.

If you do not want to use it from command line, then other option is to use –x option in the script only on the first line where the script is define. This is shown below:

```
 1 #! /bin/bash -x
 2
 3 file=/home/user1/test
 4 trap "rm -f $file && echo file deleted; exit" 0
 2 15
 5
 6 echo "pid is $$"
 7 while (( COUNT < 10 )
 8 do
 9         sleep 10
10         (( COUNT ++ ))
11         echo $COUNT
```

169

```
12 done
13 exit 0
```

Now when you execute the script, you will get a similar output as shown before.

In case you want to use debug for certain lines but not the whole script that you can use the 'set' option. You can use 'set -x' at the point you want to activate the debugging and the 'set +x' at the point where you want to deactivate it. Below is the script where we are debugging the script only for line 3 and 4.

```
 1 #! /bin/bash

 2 set -x
 3 file=/home/user1/test
 4 trap "rm -f $file && echo file deleted; exit" 0 2 15
 5 set +x
 6 echo "pid is $$"
 7 while (( COUNT < 10 )
 8 do
 9          sleep 10
10          (( COUNT ++ ))
11          echo $COUNT
12 done
13 exit 0
```

Let's execute the script and see what happens:

Summary:

Three ways to debug by using bash –x, then by adding –x option in the first line of the script and finally set option by using two switched –x and +x.

Conclusion

The next step is to implement the learning. The complete manual is set up with practical commands and is a swift reference guide for administrators. Try all the exercises from this book and do practice. To understand the script in depth using more complex logic, you can refer to the expert edition of Linux Shell scripting.

References

Author, l. (2019). *echo man page.* [online] Linuxcommand.org. Available at: http://linuxcommand.org/lc3_man_pages/echoh.html [Accessed 17 Nov. 2019].

Linux.die.net. (2019). *bc(1): arbitrary precision calculator language - Linux man page.* [online] Available at: https://linux.die.net/man/1/bc [Accessed 17 Nov. 2019].

Tldp.org. (2019). *Introduction to if.* [online] Available at: http://tldp.org/LDP/Bash-Beginners-Guide/html/sect_07_01.html [Accessed 17 Nov. 2019].

Tutorialspoint.com. (2019). *Unix / Linux - Signals and Traps - Tutorialspoint.* [online] Available at: https://www.tutorialspoint.com/unix/unix-signals-traps.htm [Accessed 17 Nov. 2019].

Tutorialspoint.com. (2019). *Unix / Linux - Using Shell Arrays - Tutorialspoint.* [online] Available at: https://www.tutorialspoint.com/unix/unix-using-arrays.htm [Accessed 17 Nov. 2019].

www.ingramcontent.com/pod-product-compliance
Lightning Source LLC
Chambersburg PA
CBHW060836220526
45466CB00003B/1127